THE HELPER'S HANDBOOK

A directory of basic counselling skills
for voluntary and full-time workers
in the helping professions

JOHN THOMAS STEWART

National Extension College

About the author

Dr John T Stewart began training volunteers early in his career as a rural pastor. While studying for his Ph.D at Boston University he worked as an intern at the Danielsen Pastoral Counselling Centre where he developed a programme for training volunteers as para-professionals in mental health.

Since 1971 he has been the Director of the North Shore Counselling Centre, a Pastoral Counselling programme serving the North Shore area of Greater Vancouver, British Columbia. The Centre staff provide therapy for individuals, families and couples. In addition they have trained 375 volunteers as front line helpers over the thirteen-year period.

More recently Dr Stewart has been training helpers in various communities in British Columbia on behalf of the Canadian Mental Health Association.

Acknowledgements

The National Extension College is indebted to **Dr Timothy Acton**, Senior Clinical Psychologist at the Napsbury Hospital near St Albans, for providing the material on AIDS. Dr Acton has been involved in clinical psychology services for people who are HIV seropositive since April 1986 and has since been involved developing existing counselling and psychological therapy services, setting up a joint Hospitals Working Party to look into services for people with HIV dementia, and also working for the World Health Organisation.

We would also like to thank **Sue Kerr** of Addenbrookes Hospital, Cambridge for her comments on the section on child abuse.

Published by the National Extension College
18 Brooklands Avenue
Cambridge CB2 2HN
Tel: (0223) 316644
© National Extension College Trust Ltd 1989
First published by Para-Professional Associates Ltd
in 1985 as 'The Emotional First Aid Manual'.

Up to five pages of the materials that appear in this book may be photocopied for training purposes. Photocopies may not be offered for resale.
Systematic or large-scale reproduction, or inclusion in any publication, may not be done without prior permission from the publisher.

Cover design: The Art Department, Cambridge
Typesetting: James Oglethorpe
Design: National Extension College
Printed in England by NEC Print

ISBN 0 86082 845 X

CONTENTS

Introduction	1
Preface	1
The purpose of the book	2
How to use the book	3
Chapter I – An introduction to helping	**7**
Introduction	7
What does 'helping' mean?	7
Why do you need this book?	8
Why helping is important	8
Who are the helpers?	9
The language of helping	10
The basic principles of helping	13
Helping as an experience	13
The do's and don'ts of helping	15
Chapter II – The trouble-shooting checklists	**17**
How to use the checklists	17
Checklist 1 – On handling emotional emergencies	18
Checklist 2 – On achieving a relationship	20
Checklist 3 – On boiling the problem down	22
Checklist 4 – On challenging people to cope	23
Checklist 5 – On special situations	24
Chapter III – Handling emotional emergencies	**27**
Introduction	27
When it's an emergency	28
How to make a referral	31
The client who needs psychiatric or similar medical attention	33
When it's the impact of HIV	36
When it's acute grief	39
When there is acute anxiety	42
When there is extreme loneliness	44
Facing surgery	46
The trauma of accidents	48
When there is violence	50
When there is child abuse	53
When there is emotional exhaustion	57
When there is drug intoxication	59

Chapter IV – Helping people with emotional problems — 61

Part 1 – Achieving a relationship — 62
Skills necessary for building the relationship — 62
Listening skills — 64
Identifying with the client's feelings (empathy) — 68
Developing trust — 71
Establishing a contract — 75
Dependency issues – referral, termination or counselling — 78

Part 2 – Boiling the problem down — 81
Introduction — 81
Helping a client to identify a problem — 84
Helping a client to clarify a problem — 86
Helping clients to establish priorities — 88
Confronting a client to focus on the problem — 90

Part 3 – Challenging the client to cope — 92
Introduction — 92
Timing interventions — 94
Helping the client develop inner resources — 96
Helping the client build up external resources — 98
Motivating the resistant client — 100
Learning how to evaluate — 102
Successfully ending a helping relationship — 104

Chapter V – Special situations — 107
Introduction — 107
A short list of resources — 107
Post emergency follow-up — 109
The client's responses to endings and losses — 111
Supportive counselling for the emotionally handicapped — 114
Working with the alcoholic — 117
HIV pre- and post-test counselling — 120
Helping somebody who is antibody positive — 123
Intervention in suicide situations — 126
Working with the depressed person — 129
Facing possible terminal illness — 132
Marital and family break-up — 134
When a teenager runs away — 136
The importance of confidentiality — 139
When no one appears to need your help — 141
The helper gets help — 143
Rewarding ending — 144

Introduction

The decision to create a manual in the form of a book emerged in response to requests from the Canadian Mental Health Association for handouts for volunteers.

I would specifically like to thank Ron Brown, Joyce Evans, John Gray, Bob Horsfall, Kirsty Maxwell, Peter Newbery and Barry Stein for sharing their wisdom and experience. My special thanks go to Michael Kluckner for consultation.

I am most grateful for the support of Ron Brown of the Canadian Mental Health Association, British Columbia Division; without whose encouragement the manual would still be just an idea.

I dedicate this manual to all those wonderful volunteers, often busy people who have been in my training programmes in communities like Nashwaahsis, New Brunswick; Tatamagouche, Nova Scotia; Annisquam, Massachussetts; Hazelton and Vancouver, British Columbia; to name only a few.

John Thomas Stewart

Preface

A note to all caring people

The quality of life in your community depends in a very real way on you as a volunteer or professional, on your personal qualities and on your competence as a helper.

One way to improve the quality of your own life is by providing appropriate competent help to your 'neighbour'.

This book is for you if you are curious about the helping skills and personal qualities which underlie the successful outcome of counselling and therapy as provided by mental health professionals such as psychiatrists and counsellors.

This book is for you if your situation resembles any one of the following:

Alice had offered her services to the local organisation that helps the mentally handicapped and visited a person who is now back in the community after a year in a psychiatric hospital. Alice is afraid of getting 'out of her depth'.

Caroline lives in a rural area where access to mental health services is difficult. Her children are all at school now and she has some interest in helping people. Recently she talked about her interest with the local doctor, a couple of teachers and a social worker who comes to the village. Caroline knows that there is a lot of support in the community for many of the more fortunate people. She is concerned about the less fortunate who have few friends and more serious emotional problems. She wants to know what will be involved if she makes herself available on a limited basis to a few of these people. She has a strong desire to get training in simple, but basic helping skills.

The local parish priest has gathered together a small group of caring people to assist with pastoral care and to provide a network of support for people in the parish. Olive and Tom are part of the group. Talking about the project at breakfast they became aware that an issue of confidentiality had become a problem for one person they had visited. The group had not prepared them for this important issue. Tom needed to talk to the priest or someone who could help him with the situation. However, he had been asked by the other person 'not to tell' anyone else.

Bill, unemployed for six months, is one of five volunteers who helps one day a week in a day-care centre in a small town. In the past year, he has been to three workshops to learn basic skills. However all the ideas he has picked up haven't come together in his approach to helping others. He tries one idea and it works. A week later he applies the same idea again and it backfires. He ends up feeling that he doesn't know what he's doing and feels that he should leave well enough alone.

Edith does volunteer work at the hospital one afternoon a week. She's had some training in bedside manner on the wards, but she's often at a loss as to how to respond when a patient starts talking about how upset he has been lately, worrying about supporting his family.

Elsie has been a full-time mother for 15 years and is considering a new career. She is thinking about the mental health field. She is aware that this would mean years of college and clinical training. She has decided to become a volunteer as a way of arriving at a decision about college. She has been told that any experience as a trained volunteer would be useful in getting into college.

There are many popular psychology books available today in paperback editions. Much of their content focuses on self-improvement. At the other extreme are textbooks on mental health, psychiatry and psychology available as training or continuing education texts. Much of the literature in both of these groups will be confusing for the helper.

This book is for you if you want to keep the personal touch in human relationships while more and more of life is dominated by computers and other high-tech developments. So why shouldn't you read a handbook, with a simple and basic approach to helping others with emotional problems. Digest its contents, practise its skills and then use it as a ready reference.

The purpose of the book

It is not enough to assume that in helping situations the required help will be forthcoming from social services or from mental health professionals. With government cutbacks, volunteers in the community are faced with doing the work once done by the social services and mental health professionals.

The intention of this book is threefold:
- to provide the helper with a resource when faced with specific problem situations
- to serve as a self-training manual where organised courses are not available
- to serve as a reference book for helpers.

The text's entire orientation is that of 'helping people to help themselves'. This emphasis on self-help is always within the context of a workable, available and adequate support system.

Professionals in the field of mental health have long emphasised that early, competent and caring help greatly reduces personal tragedy, as well as the cost to the individual and the community. The findings of 29 research projects into the subject have shown:
- that even one hour spent in psychotherapy reduces by 60 per cent the amount of medical care used over the following five years
- that six therapy visits can reduce the use of medical care by 75 per cent, again over the following five years.

While the book is not a standard text for professionals, its basic principles have evolved from the experiences of both volunteers and professionals.

How to use this book

The most important first step in using this book is to read and re-read pages 7-15 which set out:
- what helping means
- the principles upon which helping is based
- the experience (process) of helping
- the do's and don'ts of helping.

There are four ways the helper can use this book:
- as a trouble-shooting resource
- as a self-improvement resource
- as a training resource
- as a desensitisation resource.

As a trouble-shooting resource

Trouble-shooting is an excellent tool for the helper
- when facing a client who needs help and the helper is not clear about what needs to be done
- when things have got bogged down, or some serious breakdown has happened to the helping process and/or relationship in which the helper has been involved.

In either of the above situations you would turn to the appropriate trouble-shooting checklist after you have made some guesses about the nature of the problem you are facing.

Try it now to see how it works!

Here's how the trouble-shooting checklist works when the helper is bogged down in a helping situation. For example, a 30 year-old man you have been helping keeps asking for your advice, yet never follows it through. You have become discouraged because he just does not take any steps toward solving his problem.

In this situation you would turn to the trouble-shooting checklist on challenging people to cope p. 23. From the list you would select those problems most like this one. You then turn to the appropriate pages in the book In the next meeting with the client you will follow the step by step procedures set out in your selected section of the book.

Chapter II has more on trouble-shooting which includes five sets of checklists. (See the Contents.)

As a self-improvement resource

All of Chapter IV and parts of Chapter V will be useful for those who want to improve their helping skills.

The best time to do this is when you are working with clients. It is most helpful when used in conjunction with a client whom you are seeing over a period of several weeks.

Here is a step by step procedure to follow for using the manual as a self-improvement resource:
1. Begin with:
    - the principles of helping
    - the process (experience) of helping
    - the do's and don'ts.

2. During the beginning stages of the helping relationship, work your way through Part 1 of Chapter IV on achieving a relationship.

3. Once your client's emotional storm has subsided begin to work through Part 2 of Chapter IV on boiling the problem down.

4. When the client has clarified the problem(s) you then work through Part 3 of Chapter IV on challenging the client to cope.

5. As you are motivated spend time on Chapter V about special situations. There are ideas and skills outlined there which are relevant to many helping situations.

As a training resource

The steps to be used in training are exactly the same as those listed above for self-improvement. The big difference is that instead of learning alone you learn with the help of two other helpers, volunteers etc. Here is an example.

You want to improve your listening skills. Find two others who are interested in improving their listening skills or some other aspect of achieving a helping relationship. Invite them to join you in a self-help group using the book. Arrange times to meet. You will need at least five sessions, each two hours in length. It's best to allow for eight to ten meetings since there will be other skills you will want to practise.

The three of you will learn together through practice, discussion and reflecting on your skills.

Here's how you do the practice session:

1. Select a helping situation. It's best to start with one of the illustrations. If you are going to practise your listening skills you can use the situation outlined on p. 64. Once all three of you have learned how to keep strict confidentiality you can use a real-life situation for practice.

2. In the practice, one of you will be the observer, another the helper, and the third the client. There will be three rounds with each of you taking your turn as observer, helper and client.

3. Arrange your seating so that the helper and client face each other and are at a comfortable distance from each other. The observer stays at a distance, only close enough to observe and to hear the conversation.

4. Talk over the roles before you begin to practise.

The Helper
This is the most important role. Let's say you are practising listening skills. Don't get anxious about how well you do as the helper. You will learn equally from your mistakes as from your successes. Naturally you will feel good when the others confirm what you do well.

The Observer
The main task of the observer is to report back the helper's responses to the client. Be sure to include both the verbal (words spoken) responses and what you see; what the helper does, facial expressions and other movements.

The observer also acts as time-keeper. Stop the action after 5-8 minutes of practice.

The observer can be the discussion leader following the practice. Don't let the discussion stray. *Keep the focus on helping with skill improvement.* It's very easy to get side-tracked into discussing the client.

The Client

This is the *least* important of the three roles. It's fine to be yourself so long as you, a) stay with the client's situation, and b) try to express the feelings which you imagine the client would be having.

Beware. *Do not* make things too difficult for the helper. *Do not* be too dramatic.

5. Begin the role play (practice). If you are practising listening skills, it would be best for the client to start.

6. The observer stops the action after 5-8 minutes. Simply say 'cut!'. Then change seats so as to break from the roles.

7. The observer reports on what they heard and observed of the helper helping.

8. The helper responds to the observer. It's a good idea to make mental notes about improvements you want to make.

9. The client should give information about three points in the practice when they felt, a) helped (listened to in this case) or b) blocked, not helped (not listened to).

10. If there is time discuss together what you learned. Remember. When planning your time, allow four minutes for reporting and discussion for every one minute of practice.

11. Do it all over again (twice more) giving each one an opportunity to be the helper.

Warning
- Do not hurry this process. There is sufficient material in Chapter IV alone for 20 two-hour sessions spread over ten months.
- Remember that the focus is on the helper improving their skills. The focus is *not* on how well the client plays the role.

Bridging

Following each step by step section the reader will find a paragraph headed by the term Bridging. This is simply a device to assist the reader in finding more text within the book relevant to the particular topic.

As a desensitisation resource

Some subjects are difficult to discuss, and it is important that the helper feels comfortable discussing these topics. For example it is no good the helper blushing if they hear the words 'erect penis' when talking to someone about sexual behaviour; the session would not get very far.

In a similar fashion to the listening skills practice used earlier, find a group of people who are interested in improving their conversation skills, and invite them to join you in a self-help group using this book. You will need plenty of time, and at least one follow-up group, either to pursue another topic, or discuss what happened in this exercise.

Here's how to run the session.

1. If there are more than eight in the group, divide into smaller groups of three to four. Elect some one to write everything down.

2. Think of as many words as possible to describe these parts of the body: buttocks, lips, nipples, penis, anus, vagina, breasts, testes, mouth and others.

3. Think of as many words as you can to describe the gamut of human sexual activity.

4. Categorise these activities according to how risky they are in terms of exposure to HIV, according to these groups:

   ZERO RISK   LOW/MEDIUM RISK   HIGH RISK

5. Try and think about as many different ways as possible that people can express themselves sexually without exposing themselves to risk of HIV infection.

6. End by having the note-takers read out the findings.

Warning

Remember the focus is on helping each other to discuss these things so that you will be able to put yourself in the position of helping others who need it.

Recommended reading

1. *The Management of AIDS Patients*, Miller D, Green J, and Weber J, Editors. Macmillan, 1986; 1989 2nd Edition in preparation.

2. *Living with AIDS and HIV*. Miller D; Macmillan 1987.

CHAPTER I
AN INTRODUCTION TO HELPING

Introduction

This book is written from four basic perspectives:

1. The *best* kind of help is that which helps clients to help themselves.

2. Help in an emotional emergency situation is only a first step until professional help is acquired.

3. Increasing one's skill in helping is not a substitute for increased effort towards improving social conditions and life styles.

4. Giving help is a valuable service in situations where no emergency exists. It prevents emotional deterioration. As a non-emergency service it is valuable when the only qualified help available is through the helper. In these situations the helper acts in co-operation with or under the supervision of a mental health professional, who is not otherwise directly available to the client.

In the remainder of this introductory chapter we will look at the following questions:

> What does 'helping' mean?
>
> Why do you need this book?
>
> Why helping is important
>
> Who are the helpers?
>
> The language of helping
>
> The basic principles of helping
>
> Helping as an experience
>
> The do's and don'ts of helping.

What does 'helping' mean?

'Helping' is the assistance provided by people who are in the front line where individuals, couples or families are suffering emotional pain, trauma or distress (usually in relation to some specific life situation). The concept of 'helping' includes more than the idea of being first on the scene of the troubled situation.

The helper may well be the first trained person on the scene, who is

- available in a private setting, office or home
- answering a crisis call on the telephone
- accidentally on the scene in a public setting
- selected by a mental health professional for front line support
- selected by an organisation, such as a crisis centre or a church for front line support.

The helper may be selected by the mental health professional to provide extra support in addition to therapy or counselling offered by the professional.

This concept of helping includes semi-professionals (other volunteers) who provide supportive, on-going counselling to the emotionally handicapped.

In promoting the idea of helping we subscribe to the belief that much emotional pain and distress can be prevented by
- social action that helps to change unhealthy community influences
- encouraging people to adopt healthy lifestyles
- practising in our daily contact with colleagues, friends and family many of the principles set down in this handbook, such as *helping people to help themselves*.

Why do you need this book?

A revolution in mental health has been underway for a number of years now. In all likelihood you, the reader, are part of this dramatic change. The revolution I speak of is the extent to which volunteers and non-professionals are helping in the mental health field. While there are many textbooks available for the professional and plenty of pop-psychology books in the area of personal development, there is no handbook which provides information and assistance for the volunteer or semi-professional who is helping another person with an emotional problem.

If you are helping others with emotional problems you not only have a right to basic information about helping skills, but you have an obligation to know your limitations and to provide help which is helpful and not harmful. We can't turn back the tide of the revolution by hiding our heads in the sand or by a general application of the half-truth that 'a little knowledge is a dangerous thing'.

For those of you who are concerned about your lack of professional skills, there are important principles which, if followed closely, will keep you from getting out of your depth.

First there is the emphasis of helping the client to help themselves.

Second there is a strong emphasis on knowing your limitations and referring to the appropriate professional, instead of trying to help beyond your competence.

Many professionals in the field of mental health care are aware of how necessary the information and help in this manual is. Some professionals will claim that 'a little knowledge is a dangerous thing', However, a large majority of mental health professionals *appreciate* you and your work, as long as you do not try to help beyond your level of competence.

Why helping is important

Helping is important because
- of its availability when clients first need it
- it lessens the high costs involved when intervention is delayed
- people whose emotional trauma persists over a period of time are helped back to health by resolving their problem
- the emotionally handicapped find support in the helper whose help is in addition to other support.

The helper is usually the first trained person on the scene when help is needed. It has been clearly established through research that those clients who get help early in a crisis come through the crisis more able to cope with life than those who do not get help early.

The more people available to those in crises is another very positive factor.

In many communities, large or small, clients often have to wait for weeks to get help. While the crisis may have passed, the unresolved emotions are repressed only to create problems later on for the client.

While the study of personal development and emotional growth is a new science, we already know certain important facts:

- People under stress need competent help in sufficient quantity to 'help them help themselves' before emotional damage has taken place.
- In 1970 the results of a study were published in a book *The Non-Professional Revolution in Mental Health*. It is based on a study of over 10,000 non-professionals working in 185 mental health sponsored projects across the United States of America.

    'The most frequently mentioned single reason for using non-professionals was the need to provide informal sustaining relationships to patients and clients.

    The next most frequently mentioned reason was the need to relieve the professional of tasks not requiring professional expertise.' [1]
- As we move forward into a more highly computerised and impersonal society, it is reasonable to conclude that your role as a helper will become even more important than it is now.
- The emotional well-being, the mental health of individuals and families, the quality of life in your community all depend, in a very real way, on your competence, your personal qualities and your being available when people need help.

Who are the helpers?

In order to be clear about the large number of people who are helpers, let's divide them into four groups:

1. Volunteers who have had some basic training.

2. Semi-professionals who are paid and have responsibility for helping those with emotional problems, e.g. a co-ordinator of volunteers.

3. Volunteers and/or neighbours without any training who find themselves in a situation where there is an emotional emergency and they have to do 'something' until someone with training is available.

4. Mental health professionals who find themselves dealing with clients who are in an emotional emergency.

Some helpers in category 1, 2 or 3 may find that they have less than adequate training and are in situations where no adequately trained professional is available to help when it is needed. These people are encouraged:

- to contact their local branch of organisations such as MENCAP for information about training opportunities
- to use this manual as a self-help tool until training can be acquired. See p. 3 on *How to use the book*.

---

[1] Sobey, Francine – *The Non-Professional Revolution in Mental Health*, published 1970, Columbia University Press, New York and London

Helpers will find work to do in one or more of the following situations (there may be others):
- as neighbours and friends
- as volunteers whose authority, in part, is from a recognised community agency e.g. the Church, the Samaritans, or one of the many helping organisations which have emerged over the past few years
- as paid professionals or semi-professionals who find themselves facing a client in an emotional emergency.

There are not enough mental health professionals in our society to cover all the requirements. Even if there were sufficient professionals, two obvious handicaps underline the necessity for volunteer and non-professional help:
- the fact that help is required in the front line removed from the settings where most professionals work
- the high cost of providing professional help *wherever* and *whenever* the need arises.

In summary, this handbook is aimed at those helpers who are in people's homes, at places of work or play, or who are helping clients in a more organised programme within the community.

The language of helping

Some of the language of helping speaks for itself and needs no definition. There are about thirty words or terms used in this handbook which will be either new to helpers or will have their own specific meaning. These are defined below:

A.B.C.'s: — A stands for 'Achieving the helping relationship'; B for 'Boiling the problem down' and C for 'Challenging the client to cope.'

Acceptance — This is an aspect of the quality of the relationship where the client feels accepted by the helper.

Alcoholic — p. 118 provides a medical definition.

Antisocial personality — This particular diagnostic term is included because of the serious difficulties in the way of helping such people with their emotions. Many of their emotional responses to life's situations are manipulative making it difficult to understand or to help them. The 'con man' is a prime example.

Attend — To give full attention to the person, to their feelings, words and expressions, hence the client feels the attention.

Client — A difficult helping word because of its association with customer. It is the common word used in the books in the helping field. 'Patient' is too medical, 'helpee' is too artificial.

Confidentiality — A quality of the helping relationship. The client has reason to trust completely that the helper will not talk to others intentionally or unintentionally without clear permission.

Confront — Verbal questioning or encouraging the client to:
- look at things differently, to consider discrepancies in his/her story, feelings or behaviour
- change behaviour.

Contract or covenant — The agreement made between the helper and the client. It is assumed that there are always agreements, whether they are acknowledged or not.

Crisis — An emotional emergency. The person in crisis is in danger of not being able to look after themselves, not eating for example; or they may be in danger of harming themselves or others; they may be in danger of an emotional collapse.

Defensive — The person who is emotionally defensive is attempting to solve their problem in ways which are usually unhelpful; some defences are used against the help offered. Some defences are helpful, e.g. the defence of keeping a stiff upper lip when you are the only one around capable of taking charge.

Emotional involvement — Refers to the helper getting entangled in the client's emotions, usually because of the helper's own unchecked or unconscious needs; e.g. feeling sorry for, or falling in love with the client, worrying excessively about the client or getting angry with the client.

Empathy — See p. 68 for details.

Evaluation — A review of the helping relationship and process, and of the client's progress. Done at times during the process and usually at the end of a helping situation.

Helping alliance — The relationship that develops between the helper and the client. It describes a situation where the helper helps the client to help themselves.

Interdependent — Describes the quality of the relationship the client establishes with people who can help. It involves giving and receiving, being independent or dependent according to the circumstances.

Inner resources — Refers to the strengths for coping and managing life that the client has within, e.g. self-esteem, courage, humour, etc.

Judgmental — Viewing the client and their behaviour with disapproval. This often involves disapproving not only of the client's behaviour but of their personality as well.

Network — Refers to the people in the client's and the helper's support system, e.g. family, friends, colleagues at work and helping professionals such as doctors.

Process — The way the helping relationship happens. In particular it is what the helper and the client see as the helping experience or journey together. An observer of the process may be more accurate in a description of what is seen.

Reality-testing — A check on how well the client is in touch with what is real around them. Are they aware of the time and day? Is their view of events greatly exaggerated or distorted?

Referral — Describes how the client reaches you or goes from you to another helper.

Repressed — Refers to emotions and memories of past traumatic experiences which have been put away, largely forgotten, but remain unresolved. These operate in the unconscious often in ways which restrict the ability to handle current and future crises.

Resistance — The client is dragging their feet in relation to the help offered and available; often the client is not aware of this resistance.

Secondary gain — The benefits gained by the client in keeping their emotions or unhelpful behaviour; these may appear to the client to be too valuable to give up, no matter how destructive. The client may not be aware that they are hanging on for reasons of 'gain'.

Semi-professional — Semi-professional refers to those people in the mental health field other than those professionals who are being paid for their work or services. The semi-professional may be getting paid but is not in one of the mental health professions. e.g. a co-ordinator of volunteers. Usually the quasi–professional is a volunteer and may or may not be a mental health professional.

Supervision and consultation — Both of these terms describe aspects of the helper's support system. In addition to support, these services are educational. In supervision your supervisor shares some of the responsibility with you and the contract is more on-going and regular than in consultation.

Support system — The same as 'network' above.

Supportive counselling — Describes a helping relationship where the helper does not expect change or improvement by the client as a result of the relationship. The reality is that the client would probably deteriorate without the relationship. Any improvement would be incidental and a surprise.

Termination — The process of ending the helping relationship. One assumption of this book is that it is unhelpful not to deal openly with the ending process.

Triangle — Refers to relationships where there are threes, usually three people rather than three groupings of people, e.g. the boss, the helper and the client.

Unconscious — Refers to a large part of the individual's mental system, which is active whether the person is awake or not. Often it is helpful for a client to develop awareness of some of the material and information in the unconscious. At other times a client needs help in repressing old fears or impulses which seem to have a way of breaking through into their awareness and frightening them.

The basic principles of helping

Emotional trauma, pain and turmoil are not always the result of accidents. This book acknowledges that some of the emotional trauma in our modern society is the result of unfortunate, unexpected crises, such as industrial or road accidents. Some of it is the result of the lack of nurture, love and support during the critical years of childhood and adolescence; some of it is simply the normal response of fairly healthy people to natural crises. *It is not the intention of this book to focus on removing the causes.*

In the process of *'helping people to help themselves'*, there is a strong preventative aspect in that those people who have received help become better skilled and better equipped emotionally to handle their next crisis.

Getting help as soon as possible in the crisis makes a big difference by way of lessening the severity of the crisis. The quality and type of help can further reduce the emotional severity and the length of the crisis.

This approach fosters good health and can reduce loss of productivity, creativity and money by the individual, their employer and the community at large.

The principle of having an adequate support system

With the increased mobility of people in the past fifty years, family and friends become so dispersed for a lot of people that they are of little help in time of need. In addition, more and more people are living by themselves. The result is that many people do not have extended social support networks available when the crises come.

An important principle then is that the helper should do as much as possible to encourage and aid the client in building up an adequate and available support system.

Helping as an experience

The process which the helper and client go through in the helping experience is one that moves from the initial introduction to the end, in progressive, clearly identifiable stages. This experience is sometimes referred to as the A B C of helping.

The A B C model was first developed as a technique for crisis counselling by the psychiatrist, Warren L. Jones.[1] I have adapted the model and used it successfully for years after discovering it in the book *Pastoral Counseling*, by Howard J. Clinebell Jr.

'A' stands for the initial work and effort of Achieving a Relationship.
'B' Boiling the Problem Down describes the next stage after the emotions have settled.
'C' stands for Challenging the Client to Cope; necessary in going some way to resolving the problem.

While there is some overlapping in the stages, you cannot do the work of B before A, nor is the work of C effective unless B has been well done.

The final stage of the process is the ending of the helping relationship. This is covered in more detail in Chapters IV and V.

---

[1] Jones, Warren L. – *The A-B-C Method of Crisis Management*; Mental Hygiene (Jan. 1968), p. 87.

Here is a brief illustration outlining the process:

Jean is a trained helper. One Saturday she receives an anxious call from her old friend Elaine. She asks Jean to come to see her neighbour Margaret whose husband has just walked out, leaving Margaret with three small children. Elaine is afraid that Margaret will commit suicide.

Jean goes immediately. Elaine introduces her to Margaret (the client). Elaine leaves the scene for the time being.

For two hours Jean works on building a relationship with Margaret: part A above. Trust develops and Margaret settles down emotionally. However, nothing much has been resolved.

Some work was done in relation to part B above. Jean encouraged Margaret to take a look at the size and availability of those who could support her. During this process Margaret decided that she would call her sister who lived 25 miles away. She told her sister what had happened and the sister offered to come and stay for a day.

In this brief time together, Jean, the helper and Margaret, the client, are already into the C part of helping.

Jean was able to help Margaret significantly over the next three weeks before dropping out of the picture. They worked a lot on clarifying the problems (part B), as Margaret looked at her new situation. When Margaret felt overcome by her feelings they would move back into part A for a brief time. At times, Jean had to confront Margaret in order to encourage her to follow up some plan of action that Margaret had thought of herself.

They ended the formal aspect of the helping process when Margaret joined a self-help group for separated people.

They accidentally see each other occasionally when shopping and stop to chat briefly. Usually Margaret reports something positive about her new life.

The do's and don'ts of helping

DO

- Do take time to be courteous and friendly.
- Do be clear about any agreements you make with your client.
- Do try to understand what your client is experiencing.
- Do listen for feelings as well as for information.
- Do be supportive and encouraging.
- Do respect your client.
- Do encourage your client to take prescribed medication.
- Do keep your commitments of time.
- Do be trustworthy.
- Do remember that laughter can be good medicine.
- Do keep your own support system intact. Practise what you preach!

DO NOT

- Do not leak any confidential information to anyone!
- Do not make promises you cannot keep.
- Do not change appointments or be late.
- Do not argue with the client.
- Do not load the client with your own problems.
- Do not go along with deluded, unreal ideas or behaviour.
- Do not encourage or suggest the use of medication other than what the doctor prescribes.
- Do not support clients when they disobey their doctor's orders and prescriptions.

CHAPTER II
THE TROUBLE-SHOOTING CHECKLISTS

How to use the checklists

Trouble-shooting can be a simple way of improving your skills as a helper as well as helping you turn a problem area into a creative experience. It is also a good way of using this book in a systematic way.

The trouble-shooting procedures shown here identify typical problems helpers experience in a variety of helping situations, and point to the specific page in the book where there are ideas for help and learning. These are not the only approaches to your problem. There may be several approaches to a problem, but all methods offered in the book have one common approach – *helping people to help themselves*.

Begin with your question or problem. The question may have to do with a specific problem you are experiencing in a helping relationship. Or you may have become aware that it is a recurring problem. If it's the latter, you need to focus on your role as the helper rather than on the client.

If the problem is an emergency, you should turn to the '*Emergency*' checklist on p. 18.

If the problem is related to the helping relationship, you should go through that particular checklist, on p. 20.

If the client's problem is unclear, turn to the checklist on *Boiling the problem down*, p. 22.

When you are having difficulty in the area of challenging the client to 'get on with it', go through the checklist on *Challenging People to Cope*.

A fifth checklist is provided to cover special situations.

Using the checklists for improving your skills

Those helpers who want to improve their helping skills may use the checklist in two steps:

1. As a means of identifying areas where you need to improve your skills.

2. As an index to discover where there is help for you in the handbook.

Improving your skills often results in increased satisfaction and enjoyment for the helper.

Checklist 1

On handling emotional emergencies

I'm having difficulty in telling the difference between emergency and non-emergency situations.	Check p. 28
Clients resist my suggestions when I propose that they take steps to get professional help.	Check p. 31
I'm afraid that my client will think that I'm trying to get rid of him/her if I suggest going to a professional.	Check p. 31
I don't want my client to think that matters are worse than they actually are, so I hesitate to suggest professional help.	Check p. 31
When I came away from the client after half an hour with them, everything was totally confused! I'm wondering if the client needs psychiatric help.	Check p. 33
There's a mystique about psychiatrists and psychologists that's a problem for me. I tend to think that no one else should be providing help.	Check p. 33
I'm afraid to consult with professionals to get help for difficult helping situations.	Check p. 130
I didn't realise that there is a difference between acute grief and ordinary grief.	Check pp. 39/40
When is grief dangerous to the mourner?	Check pp. 39/40
What do I do with my own anxiety when my client is too anxious to look after themselves in a given situation?	Check p. 43
When is anxiety dangerous?	Check pp. 42/43
There are plenty of lonely people in our neighbourhood. I would like to help but I don't know how to get together with them.	Check p. 44
How can I get involved in post-emergency follow-up after an accident? Doctors don't seem to have time to help with the emotional storms that develop.	Check pp. 49/109
Do I attend first to the emotional aspect or the physical injury when helping an accident victim?	Check p. 49

I found myself talking about my own surgery when
I was trying to help Mr. Smith with his anxiety
about going to the hospital. That didn't help! Check pp. 47/68

The priest called me to say that Mrs Jones
is getting out of hospital on Wednesday, that
she will be alone and has few friends. Check p. 99

I've been asked to talk with a man whose wife has
been hospitalised as a result of his hitting her.
What do I do with him? Check p. 51

A woman and two children are hiding at a friend's
house. Her husband has been beating her up. How
can I help in this situation? Check p. 52

I'm a strong advocate of women's rights. I think
most men are dangerous. I want to help the victims
of beatings. Check p. 51

I've been talking with a woman who has just
discovered that her husband has been sexually
involved with their 8-year-old daughter. She
insists that I do not report this to the police. Check pp. 53–55

An older man has asked to talk because he has
been molesting his 6-year-old granddaughter.
What do I say and do? Check p. 56

A client is unconscious from drug abuse. She is
very pale and appears to be choking. Her friend
is in a panic. Check p. 60

A client has asked for help because he is afraid.
But he keeps arguing with me. I can't seem
to be able to make him understand. Check pp. 59/64

A client, 20 years old, has several personal
problems and has asked me to help. She is
hooked on drugs. Should I try to help her? Check p. 59

Checklist 2

On achieving a relationship

I'm worried about what to do when first meeting the client.	Check p. 66
The client sees me only as a volunteer and wants someone with more status.	Check pp. 141
I seem to have to do all the talking.	Check p. 66
I sense that the client doesn't trust me.	Check p. 71
I ask the right questions but don't get any information.	Check p. 68
We got together once, but we don't get on and the client appears to be avoiding any further contacts.	Check p. 69
We talked more about me than about the client and I came away feeling that I was the one with the problem.	Check p. 69
The client appeared to be experiencing something which I couldn't understand or come to grips with.	Check p. 69
The feelings I pick up do not fit with the things my client's saying.	Check p. 69
I doubt my authority as a helper. What right have I to assume that I can help?	Check p. 143
I'm uncomfortable because I'm aware that I'm experiencing or have experienced problems similar to the client's.	Check p. 69
I don't like this client.	Check p. 31
I feel that I'm getting caught in a triangle with a family member of the client or with some other person in the client's network of supporters.	Check p. 68
I feel manipulated by the client and don't know how to handle the manipulation.	Check p. 119
I'm finding it hard to listen for information and feelings at the same time and keeping the two separate in my mind.	Check p. 69
Responding to feelings is not easy for me.	Check p. 68

I come away from seeing a client and it's always unclear about the next meeting.	Check p. 76
I don't seem to be clear as to why I'm working with this particular client.	Check p. 76
I'm having trouble putting into practice a skill I thought that I knew.	Check p. 4

Checklist 3

On boiling the problem down – problem identification and clarification

I come away from the session feeling confused
about what the other person is talking about;
his problems seem so complex.   Check p. 82

The client focuses only on this one problem.
There is so much more to life and she seems
caught up in an issue that appears to have no
solution.   Check p. 87

The client thinks and talks only about somebody
else's problem (husband, child) and doesn't see
it as having anything to do with her own problem(s).   Check p. 84/134

The client keeps blaming others for his problem
and how he feels.   Check p. 85/134

I don't seem to be able to assist my client in
choosing a clear, winnable part of the problem to
act on.   Check p. 89

When my client begins to list alternative courses
of action, she runs ahead in her thoughts, and
works on the first or most obvious one without
exploring other possibilities.   Check p. 89

The client gets bogged down in tears and doesn't
seem to be able to think very clearly about his
problem.   Check p. 100

They do have a particular problem but they're
fighting so much we never seem to get anywhere in
looking at the problem.   Check p. 100

I'm beginning to feel that I'm becoming part of
her problem (e.g. I'm caught in the middle and
don't know what to do next).   Check p. 68

I'm afraid that if I suggest someone else, the client
will feel rejected or that I don't have much self-
confidence.   Check p. 32

Checklist 4

On challenging people to cope – helping people to help themselves

I keep giving advice and the client doesn't follow it through.	Check p. 64
I'm uncomfortable with the way and extent to which the client is leaning on me.	Check p. 79
The client doesn't seem to have other people to relate to or to depend on for help. I feel that I'm about the only one.	Check p. 98
The client has little sense of self-worth and confidence.	Check p. 96
I'm having trouble understanding what support is, if it's not giving advice or doing things for the client.	Check p. 13
I'm bogged down and need someone to talk to about this helping situation (yet confidentiality is important).	Check p. 143
I'm emotionally drained and find that I'm neglecting or avoiding the client.	Check pp. 57/143
I feel depressed after a session.	Check pp. 57/143
We need to end the relationship, either because the client doesn't need me any more, or I have other priorities. How do I go about it?	Check p. 104
We decided to end the relationship, but we are having trouble letting go.	Check p. 105
I need someone to help me improve my skills and to check out how I'm doing, but I don't like the idea of a supervisor or someone looking over my shoulder.	Check p. 143
I would like the client to use other resources, such as books, agencies, family, doctor, friends, etc. but I'm not very good at this.	Check p. 98

Checklist 5

On special situations

I'm having difficulty deciding whether my client is an alcoholic.   Check p. 118

My client admits that she is an alcoholic, but she keeps on drinking and we're getting nowhere.   Check p. 119

We never seem to get to problems other than those created by the drinking.   Check p. 119

I'm providing support for a former mental patient. I always feel uncomfortable with this client.   Check pp. 32/33

I have trouble with people when they lean on me and become dependent.   Check pp. 78/116

I'm getting tired of it all. Everybody is taking advantage of my help.   Check pp. 31/104/141

I've got skill, energy and motivation, and nobody appears to need or want my help.   Check p. 141

Someone suggested that I get a supervisor, but I don't like the idea of someone looking over my shoulder. After all, I don't get paid.   Check p. 143

I live in a small, close-knit community and people are afraid that I will gossip.   Check pp. 63/73

I've had an urge to tell 'somebody' about all the trouble Mr Jones has been getting into. It would make me feel my work was more significant if I could tell someone.   Check p. 139

Although I'm very careful about confidentiality, my clients don't seem to trust me.   Check p. 71

I'm tending to let people come, stay away and stop as they please. I don't know how to deal with ending the helping relationship.   Check pp. 100/104

It's difficult to do follow-up with people I've helped in an emergency.   Check pp. 109/110

Once the professional takes over, that seems to be the end of both my responsibilities and any opportunity to help further.   Check p. 104

When I'm working with the emotionally handicapped, I become impatient, take over and do their work for them.	Check p. 115
I find it hard to believe that teaching people how to evaluate their situation will improve their mental health.	Check pp. 102/103
I have difficulty in finding resources, telephone numbers, and the right professional when my clients need additional help.	Check pp. 107/108
My friend's daughter Liz, is a close friend of our 16-year-old. Liz ran away two days ago. I know where she is. What do I do?	Check p. 136
I find it very hard to face Peter at work. He has terminal cancer and I sense that he wants to talk	Check p. 132
Chris has been depressed for two months and refuses to go out, even for help.	Check p. 129
William and Mary have separated. I know both equally well. He has asked me to talk to Mary. I feel caught in the middle.	Check p. 134
Our small village is in shock because of a teenage suicide. How can I help?	Check p. 126
Joy let slip, 'I'm going to drive my car over the cliff.' I've done nothing about it and feel awful.	Check p. 128
Brian's 14-year-old son didn't come home last night. Brian is in a panic, driving all over looking for Bob. How can I help?	Check pp. 134/136
Alex was on a high a month ago doing all sorts of exciting and unusual things. Now he's terribly depressed. What's going on? Can I help?	Check p. 129

CHAPTER III
HANDLING EMOTIONAL EMERGENCIES

Introduction

Emotional emergencies do happen. The growth in recent years of crisis telephone services is evidence of how common these emergencies are.

This chapter provides help in identifying such emergencies. It focuses on a variety of situations which are emergencies because there is danger to the client and/or to people around the client.

The following emergencies are covered with step by step procedures for handling them.
- The impact of HIV
- Acute anxiety
- Impending surgery
- Violence
- Emotional exhaustion (burnout)
- Acute grief
- Extreme loneliness
- Danger of suicide
- Child abuse

Getting professional help quickly in emergency situations is absolutely essential. We therefore provide a section on how to make referrals. See p. 31.

Although we begin with emotional emergencies here, it does not stop at that. Chapters IV and V are included to cover non-emergency situations because we subscribe to the belief that the helper can provide an essential and valuable service where no emergency exists. Helping emotionally troubled people in non-emergency situations prevents further emotional deterioration. As with the Good Samaritan, it is not enough simply to bind up the wounds and then leave the injured.

When it's an emergency

Focus

This section aims to help in identifying emergency emotional situations.

Illustrations

A. A client calls in a crisis, her voice is tense and hard. She speaks rapidly saying that she is at breaking point. She spills out at least three problems, one of them being anticipated surgery next week. It's two o'clock on Friday and many helping organisations will soon close for the weekend.

B. A widow and mother of a 25-year-old daughter calls in a panic saying that her daughter's boyfriend of four years has ditched her and the mother is afraid that her daughter is having a 'nervous breakdown'.

Comments

Emergencies are classified as situations where there is danger of further deterioration or of harm to the client or people around the client. Emergencies usually have the appearance of unfamiliarity at the onset of the emotional distress. Usually there is inability to cope with some aspect of life like doing one's work, getting oneself dressed or looking after the children. Often the client is afraid of cracking up, or afraid of harm from others or afraid of losing a relationship.

Because the client and maybe all those around are 'cracking up' it is important that someone keeps cool. If the helper becomes anxious and gets upset, the help offered may well not be of any use.

As a helper, you may not have the luxury of sufficient time. In short, you will have to do your best in:

- realistically and accurately sizing up the situation
- getting the appropriate additional help needed for the emergency
- finding out what you can expect the client to do for themselves. By being calm yourself, this helps the client to cool down and more readily make use of their own strengths and skills.

It is difficult at times to determine whether the situation is an emergency or not.

- An emergency may be a situation where you are the only person at the time who senses that there is an emergency.
- The situation may be one where the client feels that there is an emergency and they have initiated contact with you.
- A friend or neighbour of the client may have contacted you or brought the client to you, claiming that there is an emergency.

The emotional condition of the client provides you with information which helps in determining whether there is an emergency. Notable situations are as follows.

- The client is in a state of anxiety which leaves them unable to do basic tasks for themselves or for their dependents. For example, a mother may be in panic but still be in charge of an infant. Anxiety attacks, sometimes sudden and severe, are the most common emotional emergencies.

- Threat of suicide is clearly another emergency situation. Any threat should be taken seriously. Even those who don't really mean it, like wrist-cutters and some people who take overdoses, may have a suicide accident. This means that something goes wrong with their attempt to seek attention or help and they die as a result of the misfired plan.
- There are some depressed people who move back and forth between deep depression and extreme happiness. It is an emergency when this type of person withdraws their life's savings and goes off on a holiday to Hawaii.
- Lots of people for whom life is going along well until they suddenly experience an unexpected loss, may react initially in a way which constitutes an emotional emergency. If a person is under severe stress and is responding in ways which are 'out of the ordinary' for that person, it is likely to be an emergency.

Step by step procedure

1. Keep calm while assessing the nature of the situation.

2. Note who is saying that an emergency exists. Does your information come from your own observation and/or intuition?

3. Check the quality and availability of food and shelter.

4. Check for information which tells you whether the client's behaviour is out of the ordinary for them.

5. Ask yourself whether the client is faking an emergency. Is it a 'con'?

6. Is the client able to handle ordinary tasks like getting dressed, etc?

7. Does the situation or atmosphere feel very strange to you?

8. Does the client know the time of day and day of the week?

9. Is there any threat of suicide?

10. Make an assessment of the client's immediate support system. Who are they? How available are they? How competent?

11. Take steps to involve others from the support system. Contact should be made then and there if it's an emergency.

12. Get the client to a professional as soon as possible
    - a medical doctor
    - a psychiatrist
    - the emergency section of a hospital
    - a mental health centre.

13. If you have to leave, do *not* leave the client alone.

14. After the emergency is over, check back in order to take any post emergency steps that may be required.

Bridging

These steps may also apply where there is physical injury and where the emotional aspect of the emergency is not very obvious.

Warning

- Keep calm. Remember your own resources.
- Do not leave the client unattended.
- Get professional help as soon as possible.

How to make a referral

Many helpers who work in the front line in everyday life, particularly the more competent ones, find that they regularly refer people to other helpers. I did a study some years ago which showed that the less competent and the poorly trained helpers tended not to refer. They also resisted turning to consultants for help in their work.

Focus

This section aims to:

- improve your skills in making a referral
- improve your skills in preparing your client so that there is little opportunity for misunderstanding when the client and new helper meet
- clarify what will be your most helpful role with the client during and after the referral has been completed.

Illustration

Elaine has been confused for a month now and you see no signs of improvement, in fact this morning she seems more confused and unable to make decisions. You feel certain that she should see her family doctor, perhaps even today. However, you sense that if you simply tell her what you think and then leave it to Elaine, she will do nothing. It is clear to you that Elaine needs help which is beyond your ability and training.

Comments

The majority of people who go to professional helpers are referred by someone else. Many of those with whom you work as a helper will have been referred.

A common problem when the new helper and the client meet is that there has been some misunderstanding. Either the referring helper did not have the right information about the new helper, or failed to give enough information.

Another common problem is that the referring person conveys to the client all sorts of unnecessary anxiety about the seriousness of the client's condition. The client imagines that things are worse than they are.

A final problem is that the client often feels that the helper is simply getting rid of them and doesn't really care for them.

Step by step procedure

1. Know your own limitations and your own feelings about 'possessing' your clients or about 'dumping' your clients.

2. Be able to make some assessment about the kind of help needed. Does this client need a psychiatrist or a lawyer?

3. Find out whether another helper can see your client. Get some idea about how soon.

4. Inform your client about details like fees, location, etc.

5. Always encourage clients who can cope to make their own telephone call to set up a time.

6. Check out the client's anxiety about taking this new step. Encourage the client to talk about any anxiety.

7. Go with your client for the first visit if this is appropriate.

8. If you are going to continue in a helping relationship with the client, it is an excellent idea for the three of you, the client, the new helper and you, to sit down together for a few minutes to clarify your helping roles.

9. Use the 'ending' procedures outlined on p. 104 when handing over your client.

10. Remember, if you take the trouble to follow the above steps, your client is less likely to feel that you are dumping them. If they do feel that way, they can work on those feelings with the new helper. You have already demonstrated a lot of caring.

Bridging
The materials in this section are related to:
- the section on 'ending' procedures on pp. 104 – 106
- all situations where you refer clients to other helpers.

Warning
Be aware of any tendency on your part to *keep* clients, because
- you are not familiar with referral procedures
- you think that you are the only person who can *really* help.

There is no excuse for not knowing how to find other available resources in your community.

The client who needs psychiatric or similar medical attention

Focus

This section will help you to:
- identify clients who need psychiatric or medical attention
- know what steps to take 'until the doctor comes'.

Illustration

Arthur is a 40-year-old man who has worked for a company as a book-keeper for three months. He seemed to fit in well at first. However, as the weeks went by, the other employees found him strange and overly suspicious. Two days ago, the divisional manager had a serious car accident and broke his leg. This is the second day that Arthur has been unable to focus on his work. He is convinced that there was someone behind the accident and that they are after him as well.

Comments

Arthur's case is rather obvious, yet the 'suspicious' client can be quite convincing. Other kinds of severe disturbance are not so easy to identify. Every helper will face a severely disturbed person from time to time. You may even be facing a severely disturbed couple or family. When this happens, the helper needs some yardstick in order to know when they are in this situation, as well as some ideas of what to do until adequate professional help is on the case.

Some clues for identifying these clients

- The helper has difficulty establishing any real contact with the person. The client does not come across as a 'real' person. Emotional contact is very difficult. Often, but not always, the client presents a mixed-up picture of their world. Ideas will not be very connected. There is a very strange atmosphere in the room.
- The client has few regular friends and a limited support system.
- The client presents imaginary ideas of either persecution or of grandeur, e.g. 'being the world's greatest.'
- The client has either hinted at or talked openly of suicide.
- The client is caught up in schemes and ventures in which they manipulate others, often in business transactions, do not pay bills, use others and have no sense of guilt. (However, this client may fake guilt.)

What to do when found with this type of client

As a general rule, bring a second person into the meeting room in order to maintain reality and possibly as protection. Also, it is usually a good idea not to leave the client unattended or to send the client off to the next helper without someone going with the client. This suggestion does not apply to the manipulating client who has been operating this way for months or years.

Many of these severely emotionally disturbed clients do not need protection from themselves. However, I suggest that you do not take on the burden of deciding which of them do not need such care. *Leave that decision to the professionals.*

How to help

The eager, untrained helper can easily get caught up in futile attempts to help these individuals. The helper can even inadvertently contribute to the client hurting themselves and hurting (or killing) others.

1. The helper needs to develop skills in determining when a client is severely emotionally disturbed.

2. Once you are certain that there is severe disturbance or even if you tend to think and feel strongly that there may be, you need to take steps to call on the professionals.

3. You need to be firm with the client.

4. As a rule you should inform the client about your intentions. (If there is danger of physical abuse, you may have to be devious in getting outside help.)

5. At all times, let the client know that you care for them as a person. Being firm, to the extent of going against the client's wishes or manipulations, can be caring.

Step by step procedure

1. Once you realise the severity of the disturbance, inform the client of your need for outside help and consultation. Be specific about whom you will contact.

2. Bring into the situation another person. Convey calmness and assurance that you know what you are doing. Communicate gentleness, firmness and show you care.

3. As part of being ready for your task, you will have a list of available resources of professionals and their telephone numbers. A family doctor is a good first step. Make contact by phone with the most appropriate person and tell them of your situation and what you want. Do not let them persuade you to take on more than you feel you can cope with.

4. Communicate to your client that you are ready to stand by to support until such time as the other support is in place.

5. Let your client know clearly what is going to happen next and that you believe that it is in their best interests.

6. Turn to the chapter on referrals and endings, pp. 31 and 104. Beneath the client's unusual behaviour and thinking are fears and stress.

7. Be calm! Do not let the tense atmosphere interfere with your ability to help. Your client needs to feel your strength.

8. Quickly get professional help for your client.

Bridging

The principles, comments and procedures in this section also apply to situations where there is injury or sudden illness.

Warning

- Stay within your level of competence. Know your limits.
- Watch for signs of burning yourself out. See Chapter V, p. 143, on *The helper gets help*.
- Do not be afraid to ask professionals for their help.

When it's the impact of HIV

There are few people who have not heard of the Human Immunodeficiency Virus (HIV), the agent which causes the Acquired Immune Deficiency Syndrome (AIDS). Helpers may well find themselves in the position of helping someone who is HIV antibody positive and it is important that they can transmit their confidence in dealing with these situations to the client, and to other people involved.

Focus

The purpose of this section is for you to:

- acquire a basic understanding of why counselling is important in the context of HIV
- become familiar with the main counselling issues surrounding HIV
- question your assumptions about how people express their sexuality.

Illustrations

Maureen is in a state of panic. She lives in the same small town as you do, and has just learnt that one of her ex-boyfriends has died from AIDS. She has come to you because she does not know what to do. She wants to have the test for the AIDS virus to work out how long she has left to live. She has asked you to find her a doctor who will do an AIDS test.

Jerry believes he has put himself at risk of acquiring HIV. This is his third session with you, and it has taken some time to gain his trust. He has just told you that he is unable to stop himself having frequent casual sexual contacts. He describes having engaged in active and passive oral sex, and mutual masturbation. You think he needs help with the behaviour from the point of view of its apparent uncontrollability, and the risk of his acquiring HIV. You are also surprised at his level of sexual activity, and find that you are concerned about this reaction.

Comments

HIV is equally the social as well as the medical phenomenon of this decade and of the foreseeable future. Its social importance revolves around the fact that it is only through large numbers of people changing their sexual behaviours that the rate of transmission of the virus can be affected. AIDS causes panic: the popular image if this virus as portrayed by the most popular newspapers thrives on fears of contagion, death and homosexuality.

Individuals identified as being HIV antibody positive are subject to society's individual and collective prejudice. Such individuals have lost jobs, friends, their self-esteem, security, and more. To understand what it means to be HIV antibody positive involves discussing sexual behaviour, sexual orientation, fear of illness and fear of dying. It sometimes involves informing family, lovers and friends that, for example, their son is (a) gay (b) in hospital and (c) dying. Not surprisingly, these clients and their families often have enormous counselling needs.

There are a number of books about the experience of living with, and caring for people who are HIV antibody positive, from those who are symptom free through to those who have full-blown AIDS. Two clear expositions are by Miller (1988) and Miller, Green and Weber (1986 and 1989). These and other similar books aim to inform about the special features of AIDS which need to be taken into account when dealing with those involved. Let's take a quick look at what the main issues are in this area.

- The virus is passed to others sexually, and mainly during activities which involve insertion of an erect penis into the vagina or anus. It can also be passed by people who share needles used to inject drugs into their bodies.

- Condoms help prevent transmission where penile insertion into the anus, mouth or vagina is an important part of the sexual activity.

- Clean equipment (needles and syringes) is freely available in some parts of the country for people who inject themselves with substances such as heroin.

- People who are considering having the blood test which detects whether or not someone has been exposed to HIV *must* be given counselling beforehand to determine whether or not they fully appreciate the implications of receiving a positive result.

- A large number of people who are HIV positive go on to develop symptoms of the virus. The antibody test does not inform whether or not anyone will develop symptoms. The reasons why some do develop symptoms, and others do not, are poorly understood. There is therefore a large amount of uncertainty associated with receiving an antibody positive blood test result.

- A lot of people who go on to develop symptoms will go on to develop full blown AIDS. This means that they will die sooner than they had expected.

- Talking to someone about HIV will always involve discussing modes and methods of sexual expression. It is therefore of considerable importance that the helper feels comfortable discussing this issue. Use the exercise on p. 5 to help.

- Talking to someone about HIV *can* involve discussing death and dying, especially if the client has AIDS. Again, it is important for the helper to be comfortable with this subject.

- There is a basic requirement for all people discussing HIV with their clients to be familiar with the basics of transmission, the mechanics of an antibody test, infection control procedures, the major diagnoses associated with symptom expression, and the main treatments.

- Helpers should also be thoroughly familiar with the local set-up, both statutory and non-statutory sector services, for people who carry HIV. It is preferable for you to know named individuals and their areas of expertise.

- The imperatives regarding confidentiality on p. 139 are doubly reiterated in this situation. It is not the counsellor's job to inform anyone, doctor, nurse, wife, boss, or any other individual, if your client has confided that no one knows of their antibody status. The focus of the problem shifts to helping the client help themselves by working on methods of informing others.

The helper has a very important role, especially in smaller communities outside the relative anonymity offered by cities. The client must feel accepted if they are to overcome the enormous stigma associated with an antibody positive diagnosis. In addition to providing emotional support, and crisis intervention as outlined in the sections on *Acute Grief*, *Anxiety* and *Depression*, the helper can provide:
- information to replace conjecture, supposition and fear
- links to overcome isolation
- acceptance in a climate of prejudice and disinterest.

As a helper it may well be that, as a point of first contact your role will be one of referring to a more appropriate agency, depending on what the needs of the situation are. It is therefore very important to have a good all-round understanding about HIV, and about what local resources can provide.

Step by step procedure

1. Acquire a grounding in the history of HIV and its basic medical terminology. You will not need to become an expert, but you will have to feel clear about the basics.

2. Check out the local district and regional services available to people who are HIV positive, medical, psychiatric, counselling, and social work, and also the voluntary sector: groups, buddies, information services, helplines, and so on. With a diagnosis which can provoke strong reactions in others and contribute to enhancing the clients' sense of loneliness, it is important to locate alternative networks, often found within the voluntary sector.

3. Explore the attitudes of local GPs and dental practitioners with respect to working with people who are HIV positive. Take note of those who are willing to take on such clients.

4. Establish accessibility to up-to-date information on research findings. This may well have implications for the clinical management of HIV infected persons (it changes all the time, and some of your clients will be familiar with it).

5. Be quite clear about your role and use your listening skills to the full with each contact. Is this an opportunity to refer someone to another agency? Is this an information-giving exercise? Is this individual checking your attitudes to sexuality, or to HIV, by speaking in the third person? Do they need help themselves?

6. Reassure your clients all the time. No matter what messages are being given out in terms of rates of disease progression and mortality rates, what was true for one research group may well not be true for another. Furthermore, although there is no cure for the underlying immune deficiency, treatments for symptoms are improving all the time.

Bridging

This section links in with just about everything: anxiety management, depression, coping with hospitalisation, grief reactions, sexuality, and so on.

Warning

- Remember the imperative for absolute confidentiality.

- Maintain a balance between your accessibility, and recognition of the time when it is appropriate to let go of the client: it is often all too easy to get over-involved.

- It is true to say that you will learn a lot from your clients; the nature of your relationship will not be expert-patient, it will be a joint venture, emphasising your role of helping someone to help themselves.

When it's acute grief

Focus

This section will help you to:
- improve your ability to distinguish between acute grief and normal grief
- develop skills that will enable you to help the person who is in acute grief.

Illustration

Alice, who is a devoted and very dependent wife and mother, has just buried her husband. They have three young children. He died of an unexpected heart attack. Three days after the funeral, Alice is
- blaming the doctors for her husband's death.
- complaining about heart pains and lying down frequently until the pain 'goes away'.
- talking seriously of leaving her children with her mother and going away to an expensive resort for a month's holiday. Her mother is not well. It is not yet clear whether there are adequate finances for the future.

Alice has three symptoms of acute grief. The most obvious one is that of developing the same symptoms from which her husband died. The other two, less obvious, indicate that an emergency exists.

Comments

Doctors, nurses, teachers, co-workers, ministers, priests or police are often the first people on the scene when an individual or a family has just learned of the death of a loved one.

A lot has been written about the grief process, yet little has been written about what to expect in a situation where there is acute grief and an emergency exists.

Let's look at the usual response to loss and death:
- There is some shock and disbelief.
- Sometimes there is a mixture of sadness and relief.
- A feeling of confusion is common.
- Worries about the future begin to emerge.
- Sometimes there is a temporary but mild inability to look after everyday matters, such as filling the car with petrol, and so on.
- Some people experience a change in body functions, e.g. breathing difficulties, loss of appetite or a heavy feeling.

All of the above reactions are quite normal. Abnormal grief looks somewhat different.
- Extreme and inappropriate guilt feelings.
- Continuing inability to look after everyday responsibilities, e.g. cooking meals on a regular basis, dressing small children, etc.
- Blaming doctors or nurses for the death.
- Denial that anything serious has happened and making inappropriate plans, like a holiday.
- Serious body disorders the same as those experienced by the loved one during the illness.

All of these symptoms have a function, often misguided and destructive. They are uncontrolled attempts at avoiding facing:

(a) the loss
(b) the emotional pain which is a part of normal grief.

The helper has a very important role to play in these situations because the longer the acute grief goes unresolved, the greater the damage and the more difficult it is for the bereaved to return to normal living.

All societies recognise the importance of 'grief work' in that they provide community support and rituals to help the bereaved to work through their pain and loss.

The key role of the helper is to get professional help for the acute grief victim.

The second role is to find whatever back-up is needed during the emergency part of the crisis.

Step by step procedure

1. Check for information both from the client and others to determine whether the death was unexpected.

2. Using the lists above, watch for clues to determine whether the client is experiencing normal or acute grief.

3. If it's normal grief, use your best listening skills (see p. 64). Follow the steps for providing empathy, p. 68.

4. If it's acute grief, follow step 3, but, in addition work on developing trust, p.71, and persuade the client to see a professional. If there are any physical symptoms, start with the family doctor. If trust is low, begin with the priest who conducted the funeral.

5. You can offer your support by suggesting that you go with your client.

6. Often the family doctor and local priest are not trained to help with acute grief. Do not hesitate in offering your observations to these professionals and suggest that additional professional help may be needed.

7. Reassure your client all the time. Tell them that sometimes these unusual symptoms come with grief, and that with help, they will soon be back to normal.

8. Make certain that the client has sufficient and caring support from elsewhere, in their network of family and friends. Ensure that there are not too many people.

9. Encourage the client to carry on with the small, manageable, everyday responsibilities.

10. Once the emotions have settled down and the abnormal symptoms have stopped, encourage the client to begin normal social activities again, slowly at first.

Bridging

Symptoms of acute grief may develop where the traumatic loss is something other than death, such as severe financial loss, separation, divorce, job loss, or some form of physical disability.

Warning

- Do not take on responsibilities beyond your competence. It's a temptation when your client resists seeing a professional.
- Remember, delay in getting help can be very serious.
- If behaviour, however odd, is normal for your client, this is probably not an emergency.
- Mourning takes time.

When there is acute anxiety

Focus

This section will help you to:
- improve your skills in distinguishing between normal anxiety, neurotic anxiety and acute anxiety.
- develop skills that will enable you to help the person who is experiencing acute anxiety.

Illustrations

Neurotic anxiety
Karen at 18, has just finished her 'A' levels. She was planning to take a course in journalism 150 miles from home. As the end of her final term drew near, she complained that something dreadful was going to happen. Through the summer she became worried that something might happen to her mother or younger sister after she left home. She was having difficulty getting to sleep and would wake up at the slightest disturbance.

Acute anxiety
Karen is at college. It's the beginning of her second week of classes. She is having severe chest pains, trouble breathing, and has no appetite. Her room-mate thinks that Karen is having a nervous breakdown. This morning Karen is not able to leave her room either to go down to breakfast or to go to college.

Comments

The most important first task of the helper is to determine whether the anxiety is normal, neurotic or acute. While neurotic anxiety may develop into an acute emergency under extra stress, an emotional emergency does not yet exist.

Most of us experience feelings of stress and tension from time to time. Sometimes it is hard to know what it is about. Usually it goes away by itself or as a result of our having removed the cause. This is normal anxiety, e.g. being worried about being late when the car does not start. We do not experience a storm of anxiety.

However, if the anxiety lasts too long and interferes with getting things done, then life becomes uncomfortable and we become irritable. We are not at our best either at work or at play. This condition describes neurotic anxiety.

Recognising acute anxiety

Acute anxiety is noticeably different. It is more severe.

There is usually a long build-up, but then it erupts unexpectedly. Some signs to watch for are:
- complaints of choking
- complaints of sweating easily
- the mouth becomes dry
- breathing quickens and is shallow
- nausea or diarrhoea may be present

- the client may feel weak or dizzy
- the client may feel afraid without knowing what the fears are.

Most clients with acute anxiety only experience three or four of these symptoms at one time. If several of these persist after the obvious cause disappears or no reason is evident, then the client needs competent help to:
- relieve the anxiety
- protect the client
- possibly protect others
- prevent serious mental deterioration.

The most obvious acute anxiety is when a person in the face of imminent danger freezes in their tracks. Such situations are not common. When they do happen, drastic and immediate intervention *may* be necessary in order to protect the client from physical danger.

Step by step procedure

1. Focus your attention on the client and try to get a feel for their ability to take care of themselves.

2. Check for signs of acute anxiety using the lists above.

3. Are the symptoms and behaviour usual or unusual for your client?

4. Remain confident and hopeful. Offer realistic hope and assurance.

5. Take steps to involve others from the client's support system.

6. Do not attempt to help beyond your own level of competence. Arrange to get professional help for the client. For example, the family doctor will be able to prescribe medication that will help reduce the anxiety.

8. If the cause is internal, this is best left to the professionals..It will take skill and time.

9. If the cause is essentially external, remember that the emotional crisis is internal. However, the approach in Part Two of Chapter IV will be useful as you give help.

10. If the opportunity presents itself, involve the client in evaluating the experience of the attack. This will help to provide insurance against panic if the situation recurs.

Bridging
Anxiety is a common emotional factor in every crisis. This section also applies to the other emotional emergencies when anxiety becomes extreme and persists.

Warning
- When your client needs your full attention, do not spend time or energy trying to find the cause. A Dr Menninger is reported to have said, 'You don't need to know how a fire started to put it out.'
- Do not apply the above steps and procedures to neurotic anxiety. This should be left to those professionals who are competent in helping with psychotherapy or stress reduction.

When there is extreme loneliness

Focus

This section will help you:
- learn how to make contact with extremely lonely people
- identify real cases of extreme loneliness
- discover how to motivate the client to build up their support system
- avoid getting caught as the 'only one' in the client's support system.

Illustration

Leslie is a helper in a small community. From time to time, he saw an older man walking down by the river. He had never talked to him but knew who he was. Out jogging one day in a light rain, Leslie found the man again and decided to stop and talk. To his surprise the man was in the same spot the next day. This time Leslie found it hard to get away. The old man just kept talking. He found that the man does not go anywhere socially and seldom talks to others except when he goes shopping.

Comments

The above illustration identifies several factors in helping the lonely.
- The emergency nature of the loneliness did not emerge at the first meeting.
- It is difficult for the extremely lonely to reach out to make contacts.
- Their support system is practically non-existent. Their doctor and the local shopkeeper may be all they have.
- Having made contact, they may become clinging and possessive.
- The helper may withdraw for fear of getting caught.
- The helper may not have skills in encouraging the extremely lonely person to build a support system.

Extremely lonely people have usually played some part (sometimes major) in creating their own loneliness. They may have a pattern of pushing people away or withdrawing while at the same time craving companionship.

They may have given up asking and reaching out. TV may have become a substitute for real people. Hanging on to 'the good old days' often gets in the way of making new friends. They may have difficulty trusting others, including the helper.

Helping the extremely lonely person help themselves requires skills in
- making the first contact with the client
- developing trust
- gently confronting the client to do something to change their lifestyle.

Lonely people need encouragement to do an inventory of the size of their support network. How many family members are they in touch with? What friends do they have? How often are they in contact with family or friends? When the time is ripe, the lonely need to be confronted with the fact that the average person has 20-25 people in their support system.

We suggest that competent helpers actively seek out the lonely because it is so difficult for the lonely to take the initiative and ask for help.

Every community needs appropriate groups and volunteers who have concern for extremely lonely people.

Step by step procedure

1. Do not wait for extremely lonely people to make the first move to ask for help.

2. Once you have made contact, take time to listen, p. 64 and to establish trust, p. 71.

3. Do some checking with the client to establish the degree of loneliness and the size of the support network.

4. Offer your services while being careful *not* to promise more than you can deliver.

5. Attach a condition to your offer which requires the client to work with you on building up their support network. See p. 99 for suggestions.

6. If practical, add a further condition which requires the client to become part of a church or community group. Assist the client in doing some checking.

7. Ask around in the community for volunteers who want to help the lonely.

8. When you find a willing volunteer, introduce your client to the volunteer. Help them to make appropriate arrangements (see p. 75) on setting up a contract.)

9. End your relationship with the client when appropriate see (p. 104). There are others in the community who need your skills.

Bridging

The special skills required for helping the extremely lonely include many of the skills detailed in the A B C's of helping, p. 13.

Warning

The longer the period of time of withdrawal from others, the greater is the difficulty in helping the extremely lonely.

Facing surgery

Focus

This section can be used to develop helping skills with the client who is suffering anxiety about forthcoming surgery.

Illustration

Helena's family doctor had referred her to a specialist concerning a lump under her arm. The specialist tells her that she must undergo surgery. It will be two to three weeks before she goes into the hospital. She does not know whether it is malignant.

Helena belongs to a family that has a history of keeping such matters private and a secret. Her family doctor and her specialist have many demands on their time and cannot do much by way of listening to her unspoken concerns.

Comments

The anxiety that sometimes builds up prior to surgery can seriously affect the rate of recovery and the outcome of the surgery.

In the illustration, Helena is a prime candidate for an unnecessarily prolonged recovery period. The build up of the anxiety will have a negative effect on the family's ability to function.

As a helper, you may only get the opportunity to help when the situation has become acute. If it has become acute the section on acute anxiety, p. 42, will be of help.

The worries felt by candidates for surgery may be in one or more of the following areas:
- fear of the unknown, especially if surgery is a new experience
- worries about practical everyday matters such as loss of income, care for the children, community responsibilities, work responsibilities
- fear of physical loss if the surgery has to do with bodily functions or appearance
- fear of death
- fear of being unconscious
- fear of pain.

Where fear of death, pain or loss of some part of the body is involved, people tend to go through a lot of grief in advance of the event itself. The section on acute grief will be of use to the helper.
See p. 39.

Sometimes there is a lot of anger prior to the surgery. 'Why is this happening to me?' 'Why now?' If the anger is not expressed and so released, the recovery and outcome will be difficult.

In the family itself there will be changes. There may be an increase of conflict. An inability to carry out everyday tasks may develop. Some family member(s) may react adversely, e.g. drinking, stealing or skipping school. Let's see what the helper can do.

Step by step procedure

1. Focus on building trust and guaranteeing confidentiality.

2. Check and verify whether the signs and behaviour are unusual for your client.

3. Remain confident and hopeful. Offer *realistic* hope and assurance.

4. Encourage your client to tell you about any concerns they have which can be relieved with more information, such as what to expect in hospital after surgery.

5. Help your client to explore ways they can get this information. See p. 95 on confronting a client.

6. Focus on helping the client to build up external resources. See p. 98. Explore the availability of home help, or other services. Encourage the client to make the contacts if these services are needed.

7. Do not attempt to help beyond your own level of competence or beyond the time you have available. Arrange to get professional help when needed.

8. If appropriate, accompany your client when they go somewhere for information, e.g. family doctor, cancer clinic, social services department.

Bridging

This material will be useful in situations where there are other forms of acute anxiety or grief before the event.

Warning

- Do not provide medical information in any attempts to reassure or inform the client.
- If the client is dwelling on a lot of old experiences of surgery, a professional can best help with any old unresolved emotional material.

The trauma of accidents

Focus

This section will help you to:
- identify when helping is appropriate for a client who has been involved in a serious accident
- identify which particular steps to take when giving help to an accident victim.

Illustration

You are skiing and suddenly come upon two skiers. One of them, Edna, is stretched out on the snow in great pain. The twisted leg looks as if it might be broken. Her friend has released the binding but is in a panic and doesn't know what to do next and only sits there crying.

Edna looks very pale and has vomited. You see by her eyes that she is very frightened. She is suffering from:
- physical injury and pain
- a condition of shock.

What are your responsibilities as a helper?

Comments

Fear, anxiety and guilt are emotions which might quickly overwhelm an accident victim. The responsibilities of the helper in the illustration are as follows:
- The first responsibility is to sustain life. Do this in keeping with the best first aid skills taught in the St John Ambulance course or in an emergency first aid manual.
- The second responsibility is to prevent the physical condition from becoming worse. The St John Ambulance manual is helpful here.
- The third responsibility is to prevent the emotional condition from becoming worse by attending to the client's fear and anxiety.
- The fourth is to provide post-emergency follow-up as a way of promoting recovery. The emotional issues at this stage include one or more of the following:
  - anxiety
  - loss or grief
  - loss of self-confidence
  - feelings of confusion
  - fear of the future in the face of a different life situation, e.g. loss of an arm.

It is important for the helper to determine whether the client tended to be anxious prior to the accident. If so, it's best to leave the anxiety to a professional. However, if the anxiety is new and directly the result of the accident, the helper can provide valuable service through:
- encouragement
- reassurance
- listening
- helping the client to take action steps. See p. 95.

The main points to remember, regardless of which of the above responsibilities you are carrying out, are:

- Keep calm.
- Be supportive.
- Don't go beyond your level of competence.

> ## Step by step procedure
>
> 1. Keep calm.
>
> 2. Attend to those necessities for sustaining the victim's life. Send for medical help. Secure emergency first aid if you do not know what to do.
>
> 3. Do whatever is necessary to keep the victim's physical condition from becoming worse, e.g. protect the victim from extreme cold.
>
> 4. Attend to the client's fear and anxiety while doing steps 2 and 3. Be reassuring. Tell your client what to expect next, and what you have done to secure additional help. See p. 42 for steps in dealing with acute anxiety.
>
> 5. After the emergency has been taken care of through medical attention, contact the client and/or family to offer your help with post-emergency service. Whatever effective help you can give in reducing their anxiety will go a long way towards promoting the victim's recovery.
>
> 6. During the post-emergency period, whenever the need is beyond your level of competence, refer the client for professional help. See p. 31.

Bridging

Parts 1, 2 and 3 of Chapter IV will be useful when you become involved in post-emergency follow-up.

Warning

Remember that your own anxiety and fear may offset your best efforts to save the client's life. Keep calm and be sensitive to the client's emotional needs when you first enter the emergency situation.

When there is violence

Focus

This section will help you to:
- develop skills in preventing further abuse when there is violence
- develop skills in providing help to:
  - the victim
  - the other family members
  - the offender
- become aware of legal responsibilities.

Illustration

Doris admitted herself to the out-patients department of the local hospital, fearing that she had broken ribs. Her husband had beaten her. She does not want to involve the police. Someone told her about your helping service and she asks the hospital attendant to call you.

You talk with Doris following her x-rays and find that
- she can be released now
- the husband is at home with their small children
- the husband had been drinking.

The nurse in charge tells you that there is a refuge for women and children in another town 35 miles away. How can you help?

Comments

Domestic violence is no respecter of social class or of professions. Domestic violence has more to do with:
- family background and patterns
- lack of ethics about physical abuse
- frustration
- drinking and drug abuse.

Because the patterns are well-established and long-standing they are difficult to change.

Violence usually involves a love-hate relationship in which the abused person has a pattern of getting affection via the beating. Hence it is difficult for the spouse to bring a charge. Going to or calling the police is often part of the fighting. The spouse refuses to bring charges that might mean separation from the offender.

Women who are victims usually need a lot of rebuilding. Hence counselling by a helper is *not* appropriate. The best rebuilding takes place in a community, such as a women's refuge.

Women helpers who have a grudge against men or men helpers who have a grudge against women will *not* be helpful to either the victim or the offender. These highly motivated helpers will make things worse.

If the offender wants to talk, it is appropriate for the helper to go to them and to talk with them about getting therapy.

The ideal setting for helping a family where violence is a pattern is in some sort of community or group where the following can be provided:
- lots of support
- supervision
- training in better ways to handle frustration
- training in better ways to give and get affection.

Here are some common aspects of situations of domestic violence:
- The call may come from the hospital, crisis line or from the victim. Sometimes it will come from a friend or neighbour of the victim.
- At the scene of the abuse the helper may find that the victim has left the house.
- Alcohol and/or drugs may be involved.
- The victim may well not bring charges.
- There is often severe psychological abuse on both sides.

Legal aspects
Under British law charges are not made unless the victim brings them.

When trying to help is useless
It is no use trying to help if
- you are trying to reason with either the offender or the victim while they are under the influence of alcohol or drugs
- you become angry about the situation
- you take sides.

When trying to help is dangerous
It is *very dangerous* when the offender and the victim are actually fighting. It is common for one or both to turn on the helper.

Where help is available
Women's refuges have become available in most of the larger urban centres. Telephone numbers are listed, but addresses are never publicised. Contact a crisis line, the police, hospital out-patients department or the social services.

Step by step procedure

1. Keep calm and size up the situation.

2. Look for alcohol or drug involvement. Do not reason or argue with the client who is under the influence.

3. If the couple are fighting, stay away and get help, e.g. the police.

4. If the couple have stopped fighting, check to see if medical attention is needed and refer to a doctor or hospital out-patients.

5. If there is danger that the situation will deteriorate, take steps to remove the victim from the scene. Go to a refuge but do not give the address to the family. Inform the police if necessary.

6. Recommend regular counselling to the client. If there is no refuge available, offer to assist the client in finding professional help.

7. Offer your help to the offender. Ask them if they want to talk. The point of your help is to encourage them to get professional counselling.

8. Check on the clients in post emergency follow-up. See p. 109. Most couples will be back in the family home once the emergency is over and the situation may not have improved.

9. During the post emergency support period, your goal is to encourage the family to get involved in a counselling programme. See p. 31 on making referrals.

Bridging

This section focuses on violence between couples. The comments and steps may be adapted to most domestic situations where there is violence.

Warning

- Do not try to do more than the essentials in the emergency. Refer elsewhere for help in tackling the underlying problems.

- Beware of situations where there is actual fighting. The participants could well turn on you.

When there is child sexual abuse

Focus

This section is designed to:
- help you to identify child abuse situations and to know the relevant agency to which the information should be quickly conveyed
- develop skills in providing help to individuals and families where there is child abuse. This includes help for the abuser.
- make you aware of legal responsibilities.

Illustrations

Wendy is eight. You are her school teacher. You have noticed that she has developed a fear of holidays and of going home after school. You have talked with her mother who reports that Wendy has been having nightmares, wakes up and is afraid of going back to sleep. Recently, there have been two absences from school. Wendy's father has written the notes of absence The mother seemed surprised when you brought up the school absences.

Dorothy has invited you to her home saying, 'I have something important to talk over with you'. She had been suspicious that her husband was involved sexually with their 15-year-old daughter Susan. Dorothy and Susan had fought earlier in the day and Susan blurted out the family secret. Her father was in the background and heard it all. He left the house and hasn't returned. This is your first encounter with this kind of family situation. What do you do?

Comments

If a child complains of sexual abuse they are probably telling the truth.

Child sexual abuse usually begins between 5-8 years of age and may well continue for a number of years before it is discovered by a member of the family or is discovered by an outsider.

Follow the local child protection procedures held by the social services department. If you do nothing you are unlikely to be 'leaving well alone'.

Society is becoming aware of the degree to which child sexual abuse is a problem. Available resources make it easier for the child and a non-offending parent to report incidents. As help becomes available for the offenders, they too have shown more readiness to get help.

The helper needs to be concerned about:
- the emotional trauma
- physical harm.

The emotional damage will be different when the abuse has gone on for months and years from that in first or second time situations. There will be more of an emotional storm in the new situations. The emotional storm may include a great range of feelings by the child such as guilt, fear and shame.

The non-offending parent, frequently the mother, will be experiencing another kind of emotional storm involving feelings of anger, inadequacy, remorse and fear of what the law will do to her husband. There may also be feelings of relief, now that what she has 'suspected' is out in the open.

If you are attempting to determine whether there is sexual abuse, the following behaviour will provide clues. Several clues warrant investigation. Be alert to behavioural factors indicating possible sexual abuse as physical symptoms are not always present.

Pre-school child

- Fear of men
- Return to baby-like behaviour
- Fear of the dark
- Increased whining and irritability

School child

Illustration A combines several clues:

- Nightmares
- Loss of sleep
- Fear of going home from school
- Suspicious absences from school

Other clues to look for are:

- Child complains about ill treatment where neither injury nor neglect is apparent.
- Change in eating behaviour, e.g. overeating
- Physical symptoms such as abdominal pains with no medical explanation or mouth bruises
- Child makes sexual advances to other children or adults.

Adolescents

- Anti-social behaviour such as stealing, drugs or alcohol abuse
- Turning to other families for support
- Poor self-image
- Keeping cool when talking about emotional experiences
- Attempts at suicide
- Daughters subject to excessive parental control.

Step by step procedure

1. Be open and honest about the action you intend to take. Do not promise confidentiality.

2. Discuss your concerns with the local social services duty officer as soon as possible.

A. With the focus on *the child.*

1. Assure the child that you believe them.

2. Focus on establishing trust and ease with the child. You can do this by asking about friends and other normal conversation.

3. Make sure that the surroundings are comfortable, friendly and free of interruptions.

4. Try to get some idea of the child's needs and their stage of growing up. Do not use sexual terms which would be too mature.

5. Check your listening skills. See p. 64.

6. Avoid direct questions that will put the child on guard, e.g. 'Why did you...?'

7. Do not push the resistant child. Read the section on understanding, p. 68. Drawing and writing is sometimes easier than talking.

8. Reassure the child with positive statements. e.g. 'It helps a lot if you can talk about it.' 'You will be okay and won't get punished.' 'Your mother, grandfather, uncle (whoever is the offender) is the one who is responsible.'

9. If the child's non-offending parent hasn't been informed or isn't present, tell the child that you have a duty to inform them.

10. If the child is old enough tell the child that you will be seeking help for the offender.

11. Ensure the child is protected from further abuse.

B. With the focus on a *non-offending parent.*

1. Inform them that the child's needs must come first.

2. Establish trust. See the sections on listening, trust and understanding pp. 64-74.

3. Watch for your own feelings of anger, fear, etc. Avoid blame and showing shock.

4. Try to get a sense of whatever emotional storm they are experiencing.

5. Be positive in your statements e.g. 'It will help everybody involved now that you are talking about the situations'.

6. Beware of making promises you are unable to keep.

7. Inform them where counselling is available. Encourage them to go to a professional for an assessment to determine whether therapy is recommended for them, the child or the family.

8. Inform them that it is usual for the offender to be offered specialist help as well.

9. Offer your continued services as appropriate until some other helper has intervened.

C. With the focus on *the offender*

1-4. Follow steps for non-offending parent immediately above. Be extremely cautious about your own anger and negative feelings. Instead, support their willingness to talk, e.g. 'I'm glad that you can tell me about what's happened'.

5. Confront the offender with the fact that they have a very serious problem and that in your opinion they need special help. See the section on confronting p. 90.

6. Tell them where they can get help. If you do not know where, you can do your checking together. Stick to your task until a referral has been made or someone else has intervened.

7. Tell them that what they are doing is against the law and that you feel a moral responsibility to report the situation to the social services.

Bridging

The above material can be adapted to situations where there is physical abuse. See the section on violence, p. 50.

Warning

Protection of the child is of prime importance. In meeting your legal obligations, go to the local social services department and be aware that they have a duty to investigate. During that investigation they may involve the police.

When there is emotional exhaustion

Emotional exhaustion (burnout) is a condition experienced by some helpers, including mental health workers, nurses, doctors, teachers and clergy.

Focus

This section will help you:
- learn how to spot emotional exhaustion
- know what steps to take to get the victim to help themselves.

Illustration

Claude works as a manager in a Job Centre. The government has cut back on funds for any additional staff while the number of unemployed has increased significantly.

The stress of the job has been draining him. He feels exhausted. He has become very negative about his job and about himself. He has been drinking more than usual. Problems are escalating at home.

Comments

Exhaustion is one of the emotional symptoms of people who are cracking up as a result of intense involvement with the people they are helping. They may be professionals, paid staff or volunteers.

The signs to watch for include the following:
- negative feelings about themselves and their ability to do their job well
- emotional exhaustion, feeling that they can't 'give' anymore
- cynicism about the clients they work with. This includes hard and callous attitudes
- inappropriately leaving or threatening to leave their job
- increased use of alcohol or drugs
- increase or emergence of problems at home
- ignoring the warning signs of exhaustion
- sarcasm
- touchiness and irritability.

The intensity of these signs together with the frequency with which they occur determine whether or not it is an emergency.

If you suspect emotional exhaustion, make sure you are familiar with the section on *When it's an emergency*, p. 28, before you attempt to help the client in any particular way. It will help to listen until you know more clearly whether it's an emergency.

If the signs are very clear and severe your client needs professional help! If things have escalated recently help is needed promptly! One of the important causes of exhaustion is the lack of a support system. Support systems can be used to prevent it. Also a good support group of colleagues is an excellent form of self-help when there is mild exhaustion and it's not an emergency.

Helpers have careers that can lead to exhaustion. There is a risk when providing help is your full-time job. There is a risk when your other work is in helping people with problems, working with the sick, teaching or working as a priest or minister.

Step by step procedure

1. If you suspect exhaustion, use the checklist of signs (in the *Comments* above).

2. If the signs are intense and happen frequently, it's likely to be severe exhaustion and should be treated as an emergency. See p. 28.

3. The most important step in helping the client with severe exhaustion is to get them to go for professional help.

4. Professional pride may cause the client to resist going for help. See p. 100 on how to handle resistance.

5. If the signs indicate mild exhaustion, (the symptoms are mild and do not occur frequently) encourage the client to get into a group of other professional helpers. They could start such a group.

6. With *mild* exhaustion, where the client understands what the problem is, you as helper, may develop a helping relationship with the client. Together, you can work through Parts 2 and 3 of Chapter IV. The goal would be a change of work habits and/or in lifestyle.

Bridging

This section will be more useful if the helper also reads Chapter III, on *When it's an emergency* p. 28.

Warning

Do not attempt to treat the victim of severe emotional exhaustion. Get professional help.

When there is drug intoxication

Focus

In this section you will:
- identify when drug intoxication is an emergency
- learn what steps to take to help in the situation.

Illustration

Your local priest calls you. He knows you are a helper. He directs you to a particular house where there is an emergency and you are expected. The emergency involves a mother and her 19-year-old son. The son is high on drugs. He is imagining all sorts of things. His eyes are glazed and he looks very pale. The mother is in a panic and is causing a scene.

Comments

Usually the call for help will come from the family or from friends of the client. These calls to helpers will be infrequent except in cases where the family or friends do not want to involve professionals and the authorities.

Many towns will have detoxification units. However, some of these units will not be open on weekends or after five.

The client who is experiencing drug intoxication may be
- afraid of what is happening to their mind
- afraid of what is happening to their body
- out of touch with reality
- unconscious or feeling faint
- in danger of harming others
- in danger of harming themselves.

The friend or family member who has called for help may be
- acutely anxious
- afraid for the client
- afraid of being hurt by the client.

It is important to remember that every drug intoxication situation is unique.

Do not argue with the client. They cannot reason. Get professional help for the client quickly. People can die from drug intoxication.

Step by step procedure

1. Keep calm. Take time to assess the situation and to think about where to get professional help.
2. Provide life-sustaining first aid, e.g. place the client in a position so that they will not suffocate from vomit.
3. Send for professional help, e.g. an ambulance. You should already know where to find the telephone number of the detoxification centre.
4. Do whatever is necessary to prevent the situation from getting worse. This may mean moving the client to a safer place.
5. Attend to the anxiety of family and friends. See the section on acute anxiety p. 42.
6. Be reassuring. Enlist the help of family and friends as they settle down.
7. Contact the client or family after the emergency and follow up with help. This may focus on encouraging the client to get professional help for the addiction.

Bridging

Two other sections have important information for you when faced with drug intoxication:
- *Working with the alcoholic*, p. 117.
- *When there is acute anxiety*, p. 42.

Warning

During the follow-up period do not attempt to provide support or counselling for the addict's emotional problems unless the addict is actively undergoing treatment for the addiction.

CHAPTER IV
HELPING PEOPLE WITH EMOTIONAL PROBLEMS

Introduction

This chapter covers the A B C's of helping people with emotional problems. It contains three parts. In Part 1, 'A' stands for **A**chieving the helping relationship and covers the early stages of the experience.[1]

In Part 2 'B' stands for **B**oiling the problem down and covers that part of helping people to help themselves concerned with clarifying and identifying the problem.

In Part 3 'C' stands for **C**hallenging the client to cope and focuses on issues concerned with confronting and helping clients to take steps to resolve their problem(s).

The process of A B & C is explained in more detail in the section *Helping as an experience*, p. 13. It would be helpful to read the illustration in that section again on p. 14.

---

[1] Jones, Warren L. – *The A-B-C Method of Crisis Management;* Mental Hygiene (Jan. 1968), p. 87.

PART 1: ACHIEVING A RELATIONSHIP

Skills necessary for building the relationship

Focus

This section is an introduction to the helping process with a focus on identifying skills necessary for establishing a helping relationship that works. It aims to:

- provide an understanding of how the helping process works when emotions are part of the problem.
- give an insight into the importance of the human need for adequate support systems in times of stress and crisis
- identify various parts of the helping relationship
- identify a list of skills necessary for an effective helping relationship.

Illustrations

A. The helper, a volunteer, and the client, a shipper in a warehouse, have met together once a week for three weeks. They have not met previously, but were introduced by the personnel manager of the company. Trust emerged quickly when the client was told that the helper would not be reporting back to the manager. They seemed to hit it off well, and for sessions number two and three the client arrived ten minutes early. The employee had developed a lot of anxiety and had made some serious errors on the job. He was new to the city, having come six months ago from another part of the country. He learned three months ago that his wife was not going to join him, that she had decided to end the marriage and was filing for custody of the children.

In the first meeting, he talked only of his fear of losing his job and the mistakes he had made. In the second and third sessions he talked freely of his family and marital situation and of his loneliness in his new flat.

B. Janice was introduced to the helper through her church. They had a couple of hours together for their first visit which took place in the lounge of the church hall. She came away feeling that the helper had talked down to her and that they were not meeting as equals. She also had a feeling that the helper would talk to other people in the church. She had no evidence for the mistrust except that there was no reassurance that the discussion between them was confidential. Janice did not go back for another meeting.

Comments

In situation A, a good relationship developed quickly. The helper in situation B made two mistakes and lost the client.

It takes both skill and time to achieve a creative helping alliance or relationship. It is very common for the helper to start with a lot of questions at the beginning, motivated by curiosity about the problem and the helper's own desire to offer and provide a ready solution to the problem. People who have been hurt will avoid and withdraw from such questioning, feeling violated, or misunderstood and uncared for. Even the dependent, impatient individuals who demand a ready solution will usually back off from such questions feeling that your solution isn't any good. They will fall back to their own tried and found-to-be-wanting patterns of solving their problem.

Step by step procedure

1. Recall some time in your own experience when you were under stress in a complicated situation. Get into the situation by recalling the physical setting and some of the people in your life at that time.

2. Identify:
   - which relationships were helpful to you in:
     - sharing your emotions
     - finding solutions to your problem.
   - which relationships were not helpful in each of these areas.

3. Make a list of the factors in those helping relationships which were positive for you.

4. Discuss your list with another person.

5. Compare your joint lists with the following:
   - Trust
   - Understanding the person's situation
   - Acceptance
   - Some real sense of partnership and equality and not being talked down to
   - Encouragement to work out your own solution with support from the helper
   - Limited advice-giving
   - Very few questions
   - A feeling of confidence in the helper.

6. The list that follows shows some of the important elements in achieving a creative, helping relationship. Check the list and select the skills you want to develop. They are covered in detail in the pages that follow:
   - Listening to information
   - Listening to and understanding feelings
   - Identifying with the client's feelings
   - Developing trust
   - Showing acceptance
   - Establishing a clear contract
   - Achieving an appropriate level of interdependence (working together).

Bridging

The idea of a two-way working relationship or alliance applies to other situations such as the following:
- a parent and child learning how to play a new game or to put together a model plane.
- a couple touring a new country, when one of them had been there before.
- the helper reading this book who is welcome to contact the publishers with suggestions for improvements.

Listening skills

Focus

This section covers:

- the helper who is having difficulty in listening to the client. ('I do all the talking. I can't remember what was communicated to me.')
- the need to be able to distinguish between listening for verbal and for non-verbal information
- the need to be able to listen for feelings
- the need to be aware of one's own feelings and emotions
- practising various listening skills with another helper
- evaluating your ability to use effective listening skills.

Illustration

The 25-year-old woman I'm trying to help just sits looking sad and only talks in very short responses to my questions. I keep asking questions until I run out of ideas and get very little in return.

I'm so used to the question and answer method that I don't seem to have other ways of relating to this person. I want information so I can understand her problem. I've met with her twice and don't know her any better than at the very first.

Comments

In the illustration, the helper is doing too much of the work and too little listening. Listening in a helpful way is one of the most difficult skills helpers need to learn.

Listening involves the skill of making yourself available to an individual, a couple, family or a small group. Creative listening enables the helper to hear and observe
- information which is accurate
- clues or symbols which provide information
- feelings which inform the helper about what causes the person pleasure or pain.
- non-verbal information which is communicated by gestures, eye movements, body position etc.

Effective listening is more than getting information and feelings. Effective listening in itself is helpful to the client, for if we listen well, the client
- feels understood
- feels cared about
- is helped to develop trust in the helper
- is helped through the talking process to unload pent-up feelings
- is helped through the talking process to clarify their problems
- is helped towards self-discovery and self-understanding.

The simple act of listening, as most people know it, must be distinguished from 'active listening'. Active listening includes the notion of some response by you which makes it easier for the client to continue to share more information and feelings.

In our eagerness to get information, we often resort to asking questions, or to do all the talking ourselves. When we do this, the client does not get the opportunities and benefits described above. In fact, an early blunt personal question usually serves to lower trust, or even to violate the client who then becomes scared and withdraws even further. The client may give the information and withdraw later, or just disappear. Often silence, instead of questions, is very helpful for the relationship. However, letting silence happen is not easy for some helpers.

It is helpful to develop listening skills which enable us to understand the client, to remember what was communicated without taking notes and show we really care. It is not easy to be listening for information and feelings and to be making the appropriate verbal and/or non-verbal responses all at the same time. Not all help is helpful and the ability to listen effectively has a lot to do with the quality of help given and whether the helping relationship gets off the ground.

Most of use have to work on keeping our biases, prejudices, value judgements and experiences out of the way so we can hear what is being communicated. We tend to hear what we want to hear and screen out what we don't want to hear. We also tend to understand the client's experiences only through our own experiences. In the process of translation, the message or information gets changed into something different from what the client actually experienced. The result is that the client ends up feeling misunderstood and lonely.

Step by step procedure

1. Decide at the beginning not to ask any questions which allow a 'yes' or a 'no'. Instead, inquire in ways which encourage the client to offer information and to tell their story.

2. When you find yourself about to ask a specific question, think about how you can word it so that it becomes an invitation for the client to share. You are wondering whether the new person you're helping has any children. You can ask: 'Do you have any children?' or you can offer an invitation: 'I'm interested in your family. Tell me as much as you like about them and maybe how they are connected to your problem.'

3. Concentrate first on listening for information separately from listening for feelings. For another portion of the time together, concentrate on listening for feelings instead of factual information.

4. After you have developed some skills in listening for information and feelings, then concentrate on listening for both at the same time.

5. Keep your responses down to a minimum.

6. After you have mastered step 4, focus on listening more for non-verbal communication. Make your list of as many non-verbal things to watch for as you can think of. These should include at least the following:

   - Posture
   - Heavy or light breathing
   - Sighs
   - Relaxed or tense
   - Hand gestures
   - Silence
   - Tears
   - Eye movement
   - Eye contact
   - Facial expressions

7. Observe symbols which communicate both information and feelings. Take time to be aware of what the client may be communicating by the kinds of clothes worn, jewellery, make-up, hair style, house, car, etc. Try to formulate some ideas about what these mean without asking questions, passing judgement or letting your bias get in the way of your understanding. For example, if you don't like long hair, don't let your bias block or distort the message in the symbol.

8. Take time to fit all the information you have obtained into your understanding of the whole person you're helping. Do not attempt to communicate any overall picture back to the client at this point.

9. Straight after the session together, check to what extent during the meeting you:
   (a) permitted outside noises or interruptions to distract your focus on the client and their situation
   (b) allowed your thoughts to run to similar experiences or problems you have had
   (c) started forming thoughts about what the problem is, or what kind of person they are before you have all the relevant information.

10. Make mental notes to avoid doing (a), (b) and (c) above in the next meeting with a client. Keep your attention on them so that trust and feelings of being understood develop.

Bridging

Several problem situations are related to this question:
- We seem to be avoiding contact and further times together.
- The client only wants to talk about my situation.
- The client seems to be loaded with feelings and I don't know how to make it easy for them to unload.
- I'm aware that asking questions may be related to some of my own anxiety.
- I may be asking a lot of questions related to
    (a) my own past experiences and
    (b) hunches I'm making about their problems.
- I ask questions and get nothing but yes or no.

Warning

As you gain skills in hearing information and feelings, you may pick up things which alarm you, e.g. a threat of suicide, or anger which may lead to violence. Keep calm, communicate acceptance and be firm in bringing some other person into the situation who can deal with the more serious matters. That person will probably be someone from the caring professions.

Do not avoid asking for help from professionals because you fear betraying confidences. You can learn ways to talk about cases without betraying confidentiality. See the section on *Confidentiality*, p. 139.

Identifying with the client's feelings (empathy)

Focus

This section will help you to:
- establish a positive helping relationship early on
- increase your understanding of what the client is going through
- avoid getting your own problems mixed up with the client's problems. The client's problems are already complex enough.

Illustration

A 47-year-old man with two teenage sons recently lost his wife in an accident. At the end of two meetings with him he seems distant and is giving you a message which seems to say, 'You don't understand.' You've asked him all sorts of questions about his situation and even told him about the death of your mother some ten years earlier. These efforts to develop empathy are not working for you.

Comments

Several related concerns are involved in this example. These include:
- the need for the client to feel that they are not alone with their problem
- the need to know that there is someone who understands their pain, loss and confusion
- the client's need to reassure themselves that they are not going mad and that they are capable of revealing what they are really thinking and feeling.

A premature effort at resolving a problem results in failure largely because the client is unclear about the problem and its various parts. Further, intense emotions contribute to the confusion.

In troubled times, people tend to feel lonelier than usual. In addition, their support system is often too small. This may have contributed to the problem in the first place.

The helper sometimes gets emotionally involved in the client's problem. The signs are that you
- tend to lose sleep
- think a lot about the client and find yourself either avoiding the client or wanting to make inappropriate contact
- get too anxious.

Identifying with someone (empathy) means putting yourself in another person's shoes, getting into their way of experiencing feelings about the situation and understanding the problem. It means keeping your head clear about the real world from which you come as a helper and at the same time getting into the client's shoes, without becoming part of the problem. It is one of the most useful qualities (skills) that a helper can bring to troubled people. It is not the same as sympathy.

Sympathy is sharing another's feelings and experiences even to the extent of feeling sorry for them. An example would be when a friend's spouse dies and you go to the home the same day and fully experience the immediate grief with them. You become one more person going through and experiencing the grief.

While sympathy can be helpful in grief situations, it does not help the individual to feel good enough about themselves to tackle the situation and work through it for themselves. Some people feel smothered by sympathy, others think you feel sorry for them, and they feel inferior to you.

Do not attempt to identify with them totally. Feeling understood, accepted and cared for does not require being totally understood. Some people feel threatened by another person having the power of totally understanding them, their feelings and inner thoughts.

Sometimes in our eagerness to let the other person know we understand, we tell them about our own similar experiences. This usually conveys the message that we don't care about them and their problem. When deeply felt emotions are present in a situation with a client it can confuse the client. Clients cool down and become clear by retelling their story. We do need to let people know we understand and care. However, there are better ways of doing this than by telling our own story. Active listening, keeping appointments, maintaining trust and confidentiality are all good ways of doing this.

When people feel that they are understood they are more likely to remain in the helper-client relationship instead of ending it at the wrong time.

Step by step procedure

1. Decide at the beginning that you will not tell your own story, no matter how much you think about it. Decide instead to pay full attention to the client.

2. Attend by listening as outlined on p. 66.

3. Attend by not allowing anything outside to distract you from being with the person. Try to maintain the amount of eye contact the client is comfortable with.

4. If you come to a clear understanding of the client's feelings or the problem situation, communicate your understanding by:
   (a) saying 'I'm beginning to understand' or
   (b) by a simple touch on the arm if it seems appropriate.

   Show that you are wanting to understand by suggesting that the client 'Go over that again' or 'Tell me what you are feeling in a different way, so I can understand.'

5. Check your own feeling responses as you listen.

6. Acknowledge to yourself any feelings you are having, but don't act on them during the session. If you need to talk to another person about your own feeling responses or emotional involvement in your client's problem, share this confidentially with another helper at a later time.

7. Practise developing empathy skills as you listen to your children or your friends; it's a universal skill!

Bridging

Identifying with the client is an excellent way to improve the quality of any meaningful relationship. Try these skills with your family and close friends. Your work relationship may offer you another opportunity.

Warning

If you find that identifying with a client wears you out and emotionally drains you, it could be

- that you can offer sympathy but not empathy, or
- that the problem is too close to some of your own unresolved emotions.

You should either discontinue the relationship by referring the client to a professional or another helper and/or talk to a professional about what is happening to you. See the section *The helper gets help*, p. 143.

Developing trust

Focus

This unit focuses on the development of trust between client and helper. The following are typical situations that illustrate the points where the client may be distrustful of the helper, and where the skill of trust-building is needed:

- You ask a lot of questions but the client is reluctant to give any information.
- The client was sent to you or was told that they had to get help 'or else'.
- You are caught in a triangle with the client and one of the family members or a boss or supervisor.
- The client is convinced that your experiences and lifestyle are so different from theirs, that you could not possibly understand.

Illustrations

A. The client has been told that he will be dismissed from his job in two months if he doesn't get help for his drinking. He has come to you for help. You work for the same company and have connections with his supervisor.

B. The client has been sent to you by her husband because she is depressed and her husband is threatening to leave her. You are social friends with both of these people. You are aware that she doesn't think that she has a problem and that her husband just doesn't want to be around the house any more.

Comments

In both the illustrations, the client's motivation to get help or to help themselves is in question. What you do to help build trust will have a major impact on whether the helping relationship will work. Both of the illustrations involve a triangle where trust will be at a low ebb.

Trust-building will be difficult where the helper does not listen well. It will be almost impossible if the client has reason to suspect that what they share is not confidential and private.

Trust-building can be difficult if there are wide differences between the helper and the client, socially, academically, culturally, in language or in age.

Sometimes the client thinks that their experiences are so bad or shameful the helper would never understand.

Developing trust

The illustrations point to situations where some mistrust would be normal. This will grow if not attended to. Developing trust is essential from the very beginning of a meeting. Trust-building requires skills in both empathy and listening. There are a number of simple and practical lessons to learn about building trust.

The most important element in trust-building is for the helper to be trustworthy. It is important to promise only what you have the time, ability and motivation to provide. For example, it would not be fair to make a promise to someone that you would never let them down, then forget to show up in time for your next meeting.

Be fully aware of your limitations, and be honest in only offering help that is within these limitations. There are limitations of time, distance and your own skills. Make sure your own need to help doesn't trick you into promising more than you can offer!

The client will not trust you if you tell them one little bit of gossip or confidential information about someone else. They will be correct in assuming that if you tell on others, you will also talk to others about them. It is usually helpful and most important to establish very early in the first meeting that what they share with you is confidential and that it will not be repeated elsewhere without their permission.

There are helpful ways for building trust when the client feels that their problem is particularly bad. Some helpers think that they need to share similar experiences as a way of getting the client to trust them. This method has serious drawbacks and can easily destroy what little trust may have developed. It is much safer and more effective to use empathy and listening skills. You can respond to feelings without telling your own or someone else's story. You can tell the client that you are trying to understand and encourage them to tell you more or to 'go over that again.'

Above all it is important that you avoid two common errors:
- being critical and judgmental
- showing shock or disbelief.

The ideas and warnings in the preceding paragraphs apply as well to situations where there are cultural, social, age, academic or economic gaps between you and the client. If you are not prepared to take steps to get informed about and to develop some understanding of the other person's life-style it would be better to discontinue the helping relationship and to make a good referral.

Step by step procedure

1. When you first notice that trust is an issue, at the beginning of a meeting you could comment on the situation such as: 'It's not easy to open yourself up in a new situation like this' or, 'It's usually difficult to get down to what hurts or troubles us when we don't know what the other person will do with the information.' If it's a triangle situation you can comment, 'We both know it could be a problem that we work for the same company. Maybe we could talk a bit about confidentiality.'

2. Use your best listening and empathy skills and let the client know that you care about their feelings and pain more than the story they are telling.

3. Communicate messages of acceptance (and not criticism) without approving of their behaviour or mistakes.

4. Listen for any unrealistic expectations and clearly state in a positive way your limitations of time and ability to help. Clearly state what you expect and are offering by way of help.

5. Check the client's response to what you offer, listen to their expectations and be frank about what you can or cannot do.

6. Think about your own feeling responses to the client's story or the way they acted. Make a mental note to check any strong reactions with a colleague or consultant following your session, before you get together with your client again. (See the section on confidentiality, p. 139).

7. Before the meeting ends, make certain that both you and the client are absolutely clear about any contracts or agreements made between you (e.g. when you will meet again, matters of confidentiality, who has promised to do what when). Offer to be available in between meetings only:
   - if the client expects to be in an emergency, and
   - if your are certain that you can be available.

8. As the meeting draws to a close, let the client know that you appreciate the risk they took in sharing their feelings with you and that you will be looking forward to your next meeting.

Bridging
This material on trust applies to other situations such as:
- bringing up children
- friendships
- as a supervisor at work
- most professional and business relationships.

Warning
There are some individuals who, by nature, are extremely suspicious and who will not be able to respond with trust to any of your best skills. Other rather normal people under extreme stress may develop, for a brief period, a suspicious or paranoid state.

It is important that you learn some of the major clues for identifying which type of paranoia (suspiciousness) you are facing in a client. Most paranoid people are not dangerous to the helper; however, you will be wasting your time trying to develop a helping relationship with a naturally paranoid person and you will do the temporarily suspicious person a disservice if you write them off without using your very best trust-building skills.

These people require a high degree of trustworthiness in their helper. You will be important to them and you will also require supervision or consultation from an expert in order not to get caught in their suspicions and lose the helping relationship. Ordinary empathy and listening skills will not work with either of the above.

There is an excellent chapter on paranoia in the book by Eugene Kennedy, *On Becoming a Counselor*.[1]

---

[1] Kennedy, Eugene – *On Becoming a Counselor*, published 1977, Seabury Press, New York

Establishing a contract

Focus

The contract or agreement needs special attention because it has to do with expectations on the part of both helper and client. The expectations are there anyway whether or not there is any clear understanding about a contract. Agreements about times, who will be doing what and what the helping relationship is supposed to accomplish are all parts of the contract. A contract also concerns commitment, promises and the caring connected with these commitments.

The following are examples of typical situations where establishing a contract is involved:
- Both the helper and the client are having difficulty in maintaining regular times for meeting. It is usually 'hit and miss'.
- Meetings end and it is not clear what should happen next or when the next meeting will be.
- You are not clear why you are working with a particular client.
- The client appears to be expecting
  - some things which were not in the original agreement, or
  - things or help from you which you are not prepared or able to give.
- You feel manipulated by the client and there is no clear contract to fall back on.
- You are caught in an uncomfortable position of either self-defence or self-protection.

Illustrations

A. The helper has had three meetings with Jim over three weeks. Jim has been very anxious and low about breaking up with his fiancee. He is confused about a lot of things and this is affecting his work. After each meeting either Jim or the helper has to make a phone call to arrange the next meeting. The helper got his days confused one week and it appears that he has picked up some of Jim's confusion.

B. The client has somehow got the impression that the helper would be taking her to dinner either at home or to a restaurant. The helper was surprised and wondered whether she had inadvertently implied that she would like to do this or whether it was sheer fantasy on the part of the client. It could be that the client is simply depressed, lonely and clinging; yet it is not appropriate nor does the helper want to take her to dinner.

Comments

In the illustrations, problems developed because contracts were not clear. The more people there are in the helping situation, the greater is the need for a clear and simple contract.

Likewise, the greater the stress and/or confusion being experienced by the client, the greater is the need to establish a clear and simple contract.

Clients and helpers always have certain expectations, regardless of whether or not those expectations are spoken. There are those expectations that each brings to the helping relationship and there are those expectations which emerge during the meetings and sometimes during the interval between meetings.

It is common for the helper to assume that the client is capable of being as clear about expectations and contracts as the average person who is without stress. This often leads to frustrations with the client and sometimes to outright blaming and fault finding. The client assumes something is wrong, misunderstands the arrangements or gets times mixed up.

Taking time to get the client to clarify and explain their expectations promotes the client's health and their skills in problem-solving.

The experience of making clear agreements is a valuable social lesson in itself. It also provides the client with security while going through a stressful time. For some clients, it is one of the first relationships which is clear in its boundaries and expectations.

Step by step procedure

1. As soon as there is some relationship established, ask the client just what they understand about why you are meeting.

2. Summarise your understanding of the meeting at the same time reporting who did what to bring you together.

3. After there has been considerable opportunity to establish some helping relationship and towards the end of the first meeting, get the client to spell out their expectations for future meetings and what is expected by way of help.

4. Then be clear in explaining your own expectations of what you are able and not able to do, about time available and how often you will meet and/or talk to one another.

5. Be very clear about the following:
   - where the next meeting takes place
   - obligations such as fees
   - taking steps to do specific things, e.g. an alcoholic getting into AA
   - whether you will be reporting to a professional working with the client.

6. After three or four meetings, be sure to clarify each other's expectations. They may still be unclear or may have changed.

7. If you are picking up anything which sounds like expectations you have not agreed to, act now and talk to the client about it.

8. Always be clear with each other at the end of a meeting about arrangements for the next time and place of meeting.

9. Remember, a contract on what will happen and when should be made with every client.

Bridging
The ideas and steps suggested here for establishing a contract with the client apply to working with individuals, couples, families, workshops or teaching groups. The ideas and steps also apply to any situation where you are providing leadership.

Warning

There are two traps to watch for in the area of contracting:

- There is the danger of paying so much attention to contracting that you neglect understanding, caring and acceptance.
- There is the danger of working so hard at warmth, caring and understanding that the whole helping relationship breaks down because of the confusion of expectations. In the long run, it is easier to be caring, warm and accepting when contracts and expectations are clearly understood.

Dependency issues – referral, termination or counselling

The contract that emerges may be for further counselling, or it may involve a referral to another helper, or it may be a decision to terminate. One dynamic that has to be taken into consideration when contracting for continued counselling is the matter of dependency. The client may be overly independent or dependent. Some clients are appropriately dependent.

Focus

The focus of this section is on developing skills in three areas with regard to dependency:
- fostering appropriate dependent and independent behaviour while helping people to help themselves
- responding to the feelings and fears the client may have about their dependent needs, often strong enough to make it almost impossible to ask for or to go for help
- understanding one's own feelings and attitudes about being dependent or about having others dependent on us for help.

The following situations illustrate the different types of dependency that can grow up between client and helper.
- The client is giving clear messages that they want a quick and easy answer/solution to the problem. The client expects the helper to give advice or even to solve the problem for them.
- The client keeps talking about ending the meetings and insisting that things are better and they can do the rest on their own.
- The client is asking for help for the first time in years, is a self-made person and believes that personal and emotional problems should be kept to and resolved by oneself. They may believe 'if you just give things time, the problem will resolve itself'.
- The client is the clinging, dependent type, wants extra time, doesn't have many friends, and even follows the helper about the room.
- The helper has been meeting with his client for many months and would like to end the relationship. The helper is uncomfortable with the client's dependency needs, e.g. that the client depends upon them for advice, friendship, etc.

Illustration

A young man of 21 is still living with his parents and struggling with dependency conflicts, e.g. he looks for support from his parents but gets angry, telling them to get off his back, whenever they offer him sound advice.

He is being seen because his drinking is interfering with his work. He likes his work and has been productive. He gets along well with the other employees. He wants very much to save his job. However, he insists that he can get things under control without your help or the help of AA. At the end of each of the first three sessions, he said he wasn't coming back. Yet in between he calls and wants to talk to you again. Usually he avoids discussion about the hangovers and the absenteeism. This client is wavering back and forth between wanting to be dependent and resisting help because he is afraid of becoming dependent.

The process

For reasons set out in the section on *How to make a referral* p. 31 you may involve your client in arriving at the first step of referring him/her to another helper.

The client may be doing so well, as you work together in forming a contract, that it is clear to you both that termination is appropriate. Read the section on *Successfully ending a helping relationship*, on p. 104.

- In the first steps of the intervention a good helping relationship has been established.
- There is some clear indication that the scope and depth of the client's problem is within the helper's level of competence.
- The client is ready to help himself.
- The helper has time, is willing and ready. At this point in contracting, the helper and client clarify each other's expectations and set the goals for the helping process.

Comments

One of the basic helping principles, 'that of helping people to help themselves' implies that there is an appropriate dependency in the helping situation and that the help need not be destructive or damaging to the client by taking away their sense of self-worth and independence.

A look at the course of the dependency struggle from birth to maturity will help us to understand how dependency can work in a helping relationship. We are born totally dependent on others. Maturity involves being interdependent with others at appropriate times and in appropriate ways. Examples are receiving and learning from others; and giving to and helping others as a matter of course in daily living. Along the way to this maturity and interdependence the child struggles with their dependency conflicts from the age of two right through to their late teens. A teenage girl, for example, may rebel when her parents refuse the car on a particular night, and yet feel secretly grateful for the 'no' because she fears that there will be drinking in the car. The dependency conflict is in full bloom.

Quite capable, independent adults will sometimes show similar conflict during an emotional crisis. Too often in our individualistic society, there is a tendency to stay away from help for emotional crises for fear of being seen as dependent, weak or sick.

Newly trained counsellors and helpers tend to avoid getting supervision or help with a troublesome situation or with their own feelings of emotional exhaustion or fatigue, because of their fear of being seen as weak.

The client may settle into a helping relationship where appropriate dependency is evident. As the client moves towards better emotional health, considerable independence may be expressed. Like the teenager, the client needs to express independence as part of becoming interdependent with their support system.

Step by step procedure

1. In any new helping situation, it is important to try to gauge the client's dependency feelings towards you and the helping situation. Try to gauge this by the way the client goes about asking for help, by things the client says, by mannerisms and expectations. The average depressed client may begin by being very dependent. A compulsive, somewhat anxious, super performer may be quite independent.

2. In either case, respond to the dependency by accepting the client's position and let them know that it is all right to feel that way for now.

3. As trust develops, gradually explain to the independent client that one of the reasons they have been having such difficulty with emotions and/or problems may be the result of trying too hard to work things through alone. Explain that this is an area of life where self-reliance can be a handicap. At the same time be sure to support any stoic approach to life which the client values. A stoic approach to life, which includes appropriate dependency, is to be highly valued.

4. Very early in the helping relationship, let the dependent client know that you are available as contracted, that you will provide emotional support, but that you cannot do their work for them and that you do not have any magic solutions.

5. As the relationship develops, from time to time check with your clients how they see and feel about the dependent side of the relationship. Give clients encouragement in any moves they make towards more appropriate dependency behaviour.

6. Think about your own feelings on having a client dependent upon you.

7. Check whether or not you have need for clients to be dependent on you in inappropriate ways and amounts.

8. Check whether you feel free to turn to a supervisor or worker in mental health in seeking help with the client.

Bridging

The comments in this session about dependency, its conflicts and its appropriateness, may also apply to the helper in relation to getting supervision, using consultation or to referring clients to other helpers.

Warning

Some of the above steps do not apply to people who need an unusual amount of dependency just to function in their job or in life.

Supportive counselling may include a lot of dependency on the part of a client who is retarded or just out after many years in the hospital. The principle of 'helping people to help themselves' still applies in the supportive relationship.

Giving information may be different from offering advice to the dependent client. It is important to make the distinction. Giving information which is not being requested or which the client could easily obtain by going to the library or to their bank, may be detrimental to growth and health.

PART 2: BOILING THE PROBLEM DOWN

Introduction

Focus

This section will help you in:

- understanding the relationship between emotions, support systems and problem identification/clarification
- understanding the role of the helper in boiling the problem down
- identifying a list of skills necessary for effectively helping a client with problem identification and clarification.

Illustrations

A. *A situation which is going well.*

Alice is a 45-year-old single parent. Her son, 23 and daughter, 20 are both about to move out. Recently she has become very anxious. This is your third meeting with her. Talking with you has helped her to calm down. In this third session she has cried less and you are helping her to talk in a coherent way about such things as how she has always had people around her at home, how she has depended on the family for her social life, how much she has enjoyed her job and the people she has met through the job. She has also talked about her part in the forthcoming wedding of her son, which she approves of. The various parts of her problem are becoming clearer to you.

B. A *situation where confusion is widespread in spite of all your efforts at clarification.*

Jim is 62 and has worked for the same company for 20 years. His foreman has noticed recently that the quality of his work has slipped and that Jim seems depressed. The helping relationship appears to be well-established and he has been on time for each meeting. This is the third session. He has talked about several problems he has at work and in his home life. Your efforts have been to pick up on any problem which appears important to him and to try to explain to him what is likely to be depressing him. Both of you are getting more and more confused as the meeting nears its end.

Comments

In illustration A above, the client is being helped to identify and clarify their problem. In situation B, both the client and the helper are bogged down because the helper is not equipped to help with the problem clarification.

Using our model of helping people to help themselves requires, among other skills:

- knowledge of how to identify and clarify problems
- a commitment to helping the client to identify and clarify the problem without doing the work for the client
- being able to know quickly what the client needs, yet having the ability to *keep your ideas to yourself*, while helping the client to do their own clarification.

Occasionally in emergencies, you will need to come to your own conclusions. If the problem is confusing you, talk things over with another skilled person, providing there is time. You will then need to inform the client of your conclusions about the problem and what action you plan to take. Emergencies exist when clients are not capable of protecting themselves, or when other people have to be protected from them. You do not need to be totally clear about the client's problem(s) when you refer to a professional. It does help if you are clear about why you are referring. For most helpers, it's easier to come to your own conclusions about the client's problem than it is to help the client in identifying and clarifying the problem for themselves.

Step by step procedure

1. Recall having watched a small child of three working on a toy workbench or similar toy where problem-solving is involved. Note the child's need to find out for himself/herself. Note also the different ways in which the parent was helpful, as well as ways which were not helpful to the child.

2. Recall a time in your own life when you were faced with a major problem which was stressful for you and which was resolved in the end.
   - Note how you went about clarifying your problem:
     - what information you got
     - where you got the information
     - with whom you shared the problem.
   - Make a list of of who was helpful and who was not.
   - Recall how much you did for yourself in the experience and list your points.

3. Share your lists and findings with another person and make a joint list of skills necessary in helping the client with problem clarification.

4. Compare your joint list with mine:
   - Being genuinely curious about the client's problem. Asking for clarification.
   - Accepting the client's confusion and sharing your own difficulty in understanding.
   - Helping the client to focus on identifiable parts of the problem.
   - Helping the client to understand who owns the various parts of the problem.
   - Helping the client when past experiences or strong emotional feelings may be distorting their understanding of the problem.
   - Encouraging the client to get more accurate information thus leading to clarity about reality.
   - Encouraging the client to tell you about the problem from a different perspective or point of view.
   - Helping the client to understand that their usual response to a stressful problem, e.g. drinking, is an ineffective way of solving the problem.

Bridging

The material in this section may be useful wherever problem-solving is involved, such as teaching, bringing up children or supervision.

Warning

This session is an introduction to identifying and learning the skills necessary in helping a client with problem identification and clarification.

These step by step procedures are not for use with clients.

Helping a client to identify a problem

Focus

This section will help you to:
- identify the appropriate time to begin helping the client with problem identification and clarification.
- distinguish between the easier tasks of getting information and the tasks of helping with problem identification
- identify patterns, games or defences the client may be using to avoid looking at or admitting the problem
- apply specific skills which facilitate problem identification.

Illustration

Bill is a volunteer helper on a counselling project for drug addicts. At work, he is a trouble-shooter with a regional computer sales firm where he focuses on getting new equipment running smoothly. He's not doing too well as a helper. Clients feel that Bill has a lot of questions which don't work. In the first meeting, Bill tends to go after information and immediately to begin working on the client's solution.

The client claims that Bill's not realistic and that he doesn't understand. The client does not return for further meetings.

Comments

There are a number of factors which make it difficult for clients to identify their problems. One or more of the following factors may be at work:
- The intensity of the emotions leave the client confused and often take so much energy that there is none left for clear thinking. The intensity of the emotions may lead the client to think that they are going mad and losing control. The resulting fear increases the emotional burden.
- The pressures which are external to the client's emotional system may be coming from various sources and the client may feel bombarded and unable to focus on any one of those pressures.
- One common factor when under stress is to blame others. This 'blaming' distorts and denies one's own part in the problem and results in spending one's energy in the wrong place and in futile efforts.
- The client's part in creating the problem may be so alarming to the client that they find it almost impossible to confront it. This is particularly the case where anger, denial or guilt feelings are part of the client's problem.
- The client may be attempting to solve or deny the problem through the use of alcohol or drugs. This creates further confusion and inability to identify the problem.
- The client may have very few problem-solving skills and some training may be helpful. However, unless the emotional aspects of the problem are attended to, most of the usual problem identification skills taught in industry or organisations will not work. Having attended to the emotional burden and the client's patterns of responding to stress (e.g. denying, blaming) then the usual problem identification skills will be helpful.

Step by step procedure

1. Check your sense of whether the helping relationship is established sufficiently to allow you and the client to move into problem identification and clarification. Is there trust? Is there a contract? Does the client feel that you understand them.

2. Note whether the client has settled down, is less depressed and is ready to work on problem identification and their part in the problem. You may be right in thinking that it's the problem(s) which is causing the anxiety, confusion or depression. Hence you may feel an urge to get on with getting rid of the cause. However, your impatience may become a major obstacle and good timing is critical. Too much haste could lead to failure, increased anxiety or depression. On the other hand, wallowing around and avoiding the problem for too long could mean that you, the helper, become part of the client's methods of avoiding the problem.

3. Assuming the time is now, begin to move towards problem identification with some reference to the problems you've talked about. Express your need to be clearer about just what the problem is, e.g. 'You've talked about a number of things which are upsetting you. I'm curious and feel a need to be clearer myself about the problem and what's at the root of it. I wonder if we could begin exploring it together.' As part of this step, you might try some of the following, depending on the extent of the client's confusion and tendency to avoid the problem.
   - Ask the client to put themselves in the shoes of some more objective person in the family or network and to tell you about the problem from where that person sits, e.g. 'What do you think your brother would say is the problem?'
   - Encourage the client to try to identify what feelings emerge or what usual patterns of behaviour take place whenever they think about the problem.

4. Suggest to the client that one reason they are caught in the problem is because they have failed to look at the problem from other angles. Encourage the client to move from vague to specific descriptions of the problem or its parts.

5. When the client continues to be vague or is bringing up several unrelated issues, like blaming someone else, use a technique like, 'I'm still not very clear about what the problem is; let's run through it again'.

Bridging

Although the suggested steps and illustrations in this section focus on helping an individual, couple or family, much of the material in this section is useful in other settings.
- It can be used by the helpers in working on their own confusion or anxiety about a problem or as a starting point in finding a solution to a personal or work problem. This applies to situations where you are the helper and are confused or anxious about the situation.
- The theory and practical skills are useful in working with groups.
- The material can be used when applied to improving productivity and atmosphere in an organisation or corporation.
- It can be used by parents, teachers and supervisors.

Warning

When a client is confused and extremely emotional, *do not pressure* them to identify their problem. Be gentle and supportive. Watch out for your own low tolerance of not knowing what the problem is.

Helping a client to clarify a problem

Focus

This section focuses on:
- how to be helpful to a client in clarifying the problem by identifying its various parts
- how to help by identifying who owns the various parts of the problem
- how to help the client understand which parts of the problem may be open to resolution and which parts of the problem may be beyond any power which the client possesses.

Illustration

Nigel knows that his problem is his unhappiness in his marriage and in particular that he has been disappointed from the beginning because his wife neither wants to have children nor is interested in adopting. He has been dealing with his disappointment by drinking excessively. This in turn has affected his work. He persists in talking about his wife never being at home and seems to think that all his problems would be solved if she gave up her evening course and her bridge club.

Comments

Even after much of the emotional burden has been dissipated and the client has identified the basic problem there is often a lot of vagueness about the problem. The reasons for the vagueness may be one or more of those listed in the previous section on identification.

One of the major challenges in problem clarification is to get the client to take ownership of the problem; to confirm that they are part of the problem no matter how many terrible things others may be doing.

During stressful times, some individuals tend to become emotionally involved in problems which belong to someone else. (Some people do it as a way of life.) Often the individual worries about the problem as though it were their own. A more common trait is that of not being able to be objective about who owns what part of the problem. Lots of problems involve colleagues at work, family members or lovers. It helps, for reasons to be outlined in the paragraphs below, if the client can see which problem and what part of the problem is their own, which belongs to another person in the family or work situation and which are jointly owned by any two or more people in the system.

For example, a family finds itself in serious turmoil because they cannot decide on when to take a family camping trip. Both parents work and their regular holiday times don't match. Getting a change of holiday times are problems owned individually by Mum and Dad. The individuals *are powerless* in terms of solving the other person's problem. Each will have to negotiate with their own employer. Any happy solution will be difficult unless Mum and Dad accept their individual responsibility for that part of the family problem.

Problems are easier to understand and offer some hope of solution when the client boils the problem down into a number of specific parts.
- This procedure provides opportunity for the client to take a first small and winnable step towards a solution; successful action leads to both hope and improved self-esteem.
- The process of boiling the problem down helps further in that the clarity often permits working on more than one problem, or part of the problem, at the same time.

Step by step procedure

1. Encourage the client to tell their story; be curious and when it sounds vague, voice your difficulty in understanding.

2. Ask the client to retell those parts which are vague and request that they tell it from a different perspective.

3. Do some 'reality-testing' with the client. Ask for specific details about times and places.

4. Offer to work together at clarifying the various parts of the problem. State one part you see clearly and ask for other parts which they can identify. Continue to take it in turn identifying parts. Don't carry this too far, only long enough to tease out the major parts.

5. Encourage the client to identify ownership. Divide the ownership list into three sections. Those parts which are owned by others, those which the client owns (push for ownership where there is obvious denial or avoidance) and those which are owned jointly.

6. Assist the client in understanding that they have considerable power over those parts of the problem they own and little power to resolve others' problems which may be connected to the problem.

7. Encourage the client by building some realistic hope. Point out that by boiling the problem down they are getting into a position to select priorities and to tackle some winnable part of the total problem.

Bridging

This material can also be useful to helpers in working on their own personal problems.

It can be used with individuals or groups to help increase productivity and/or job satisfaction.

It can be used by parents, teachers and supervisors.

Warning

Be careful not to do the client's work. Wait for the client's readiness to take the steps.

Helping clients to establish priorities

This section can be used to learn methods of helping a client to understand the importance of working on appropriate and winnable solutions to their problem(s).

Focus

This section covers:
- helping the client to develop realistic hope
- helping clients let go of barriers to solutions, barriers which are beyond their power to change
- preparing the client for eventual selection of some part of the problem to work on where success is fairly certain
- supporting the client when old or new emotions emerge, threatening the client's ability to take action steps.

Illustration

Elizabeth has been irritable and angry for the past four months. There have been some minor behavioural problems with a teenage daughter at home. However, the irritability began about a month after a new department head came to Elizabeth's place of work. This man reminds her of her father, with whom Elizabeth fought most of the time when she was in her teens. Elizabeth has been going out of her way to prove the department head wrong. She gets caught occasionally in a power struggle with her ex-husband over their daughter.

Comments

The patterns people develop in their efforts to solve their problems are sometimes ineffective or downright destructive. These patterns may have been first learned in childhood and are weighed down with old emotions which are often deep-seated and difficult to dislodge, just like Elizabeth's in the illustration above. People cannot safely give up old patterns without better self-understanding and then discovering some new pattern to replace the old one.

Discouragement is often a big part of the problem when people go for help. Boiling the problem down into parts, discovering that some of their old efforts at solutions may be wasted energy, and being told that more effective patterns may be available to them, becomes a source of hope.

When clients clarify the different parts of the problem, they can be helped to reclaim control. They are then able to work on those parts of the problem which are theirs, which they are able to control. In other words, they can select those parts of the problem which promise some real hope for success.

Sometimes, during the process of boiling the problem down, clients find themselves temporarily flooded with emotions again. This may develop simply as a result of telling the story again. Acceptance of these feelings, together with some realistic encouragement and gentle confrontation, will usually help the client to get through this emotional flooding.

Most emotionally troubled people find reassurance from the helper's role of making them face the reality of their situation. It is at this point in the helping relationship that the client needs to establish the priorities. The client must consider which parts of the problem they wish most to resolve. A session on challenging the client to take first steps towards a solution is found on pp. 92-93.

Step by step procedure

1. Report back to the client by summarising the different parts of the problem they have clarified for you.

2. Check with the client asking if there is any significant part of the problem which has been overlooked.

3. Ask the client to list for you different things they have done in the past in attempts to solve the problem(s). Listen for the patterns which worked, as well as for those which did not.

4. Gently confront the client pointing out the ineffective pattern, while offering your own opinion that there may be more effective ways you can discover together.

5. If the client has been working on parts of the problem that are beyond their control, encourage them to focus on areas where they have more control over the outcome of their efforts.

6. Avoid determining your own thoughts about the best solution to the problem.

7. Have the client make a list of the various parts of the problem and then put priorities to each part, giving the highest priorities to those parts which promise successful solution.

8. Turn to p. 94 for more on challenging the client to take action.

Bridging
These materials may be useful for parents, teachers and supervisors.

They apply to group and other organisational situations.

Warning
Avoid imposing *your* priorities on the client and mapping out a set of steps for them to follow. Even if you 'know' the best solution, do not weaken the client by doing their work.

Confronting a client to focus on the problem

Focus

This section is designed to:
- serve as an introduction to the place of confrontation in helping people to help themselves
- help you to learn how to apply the skill of confrontation in assisting with problem clarification.

Illustration

Dave's excessive drinking has been his way of avoiding the unhappiness in his marriage. Both his wife and his foreman have been complaining about his drinking. He has come to you because he is in real danger of losing his job. A major factor in helping Dave will be a successful confrontation about his excessive drinking.

Comments

As you proceed through these chapters, you will realise that empathy and emotional support are often of little help by themselves. It is one thing for a parent to kiss the bump on the child's forehead to 'make it better', however, it is an entirely different matter to spend hours with a client who continues to complain about other people, or who avoids the problem by drinking or some other form of opting out.

There is another type of client for whom all the support in the world will make little difference: the person who gets secondary gain from having the problem; a client may not want to give up the problem even though they are going through the motions of getting help. A good example is the chronically depressed person who has learned to turn their problems to their advantage. They manipulate others to feel sorry for them and allow them to be dependent.

Confrontation becomes a necessary and delicate skill in all of the above situations. In developing a relationship, confrontation which comes too early will drive the client away. The client will either stop getting help altogether or will go to someone else who 'understands them better'.

On the other hand, if the helper is too soft, the client will soon put most of their energy into manipulation and/or avoidance. As soon as there is some basic trust in the helping relationship and the client has simmered down, it is time to begin gentle confrontation.

Confrontation usually does not begin until the problem clarification stage of helping. One exception is the alcoholic who needs to be told in the first session that neither you nor any other counsellor can help them with emotional problems if they come to the session having been drinking.

The basic functions of confrontation are:
- to get the client to face up to reality
- to point out the ineffective, or even destructive patterns the client is using to solve their problem.

Step by step procedure

1. Take time to make certain that the issue or problem you are about to point out to the client is clear to you. (If you are not certain, check with a colleague or consultant before confronting the client.)

2. Check your own interest or motives for using confrontation. Are you angry with the client? Are you trying to point out their 'stupidity'? Maybe you just want to show the client how tough you are or to teach them a lesson.

3. Be gentle and supportive, yet firm when you confront. Try something like: 'I've noticed that you use a lot of energy blaming your wife for your problem and seldom focus on your part in it. You would have a lot more success if you were to focus on yourself.' Or you might try; 'I've noticed tears several times as you talk about the disappointment in your marriage, and then you start talking about something else. There must be a lot of feeling behind these tears. Maybe we're getting close to something important.'

4. Be clear about what you can and cannot do in helping the client by way of focusing on the problem. Be firm where the avoidance involves patterns which are destructive, like drinking. Present your position clearly and in a way that invites co-operation and offers support. Do not threaten or punish.

5. Since clients usually need their defensive patterns to keep their sanity, do not strip away their defences. They will need their old pattern if they cannot replace it or else they will not be able to cope at all. Gently confront the client to do the work outlined in the two previous sections.

6. Check with yourself to see whether you are ready to be a supportive ally as the client faces the pain and reality of their actions.

7. Take your time. There is a danger at this stage of helping, of doing too much of the client's work.

Bridging

This material on confrontation may be particularly useful in helping alcoholics, certain depressed and/or dependent people, and with people who manipulate others into taking care of them and/or feeling sorry for them.

It can be used also in more normal situations where bringing up children, teaching or supervision are involved.

Warning

Do not confuse confronting a client to own and face their problem with the kind of confrontation necessary in challenging a client to take action steps. It is premature to confront for action on a problem that is neither owned by, nor clear to, the client.

PART 3: CHALLENGING THE CLIENT TO COPE

Introduction

Challenging the client to cope is not effective until the problem or issue has been clarified by the client and the parts of the problem have been listed in order of priority.

Common traps in the helping process include the suggestion of possible solutions too early, or encouraging the client to select a goal prematurely before the emotional turmoil has settled down or before the problem is clear.

The second section in this part is on skills for timing your challenge to the client to take action steps. The third section focuses on helping the client to discover, assess and build up their own inner resources. The fourth section focuses on helping the client to build up external resources through a support system of family, friends, etc. The fifth section focuses on motivating the resistant client. The sixth section deals with the importance of evaluation as a way of helping the client.

In summary: there is more to helping than listening and supporting. It is possible for both the helper and the client to get stuck in a relationship that consists merely of sympathetic listening. Assisting the client in defining the problem(s) and challenging the client to begin a workable course of action, to make possible changes, is an important part of the helping relationship.

Timing interventions which challenge the client to take action steps requires some understanding of the problem-solving and decision-making process. You do not need a text book or university degree to understand the process. You have been through it many times yourself.

Timing interventions which challenge the client to cope are important in aiding the client's growth and progress. Clients in emotional difficulties are usually open to change once the emotional turmoil settles down. One has only to observe small children in how they try, risk and learn new activities, such as walking, to get some sense of the importance of timing. Adults, including helpers, will often short circuit the process through poor timing.

Plenty of helpers who have learned to listen well, often wish that there were something more they could do to get out of the rut they have formed with the client.

There are helpers who get caught in a very different trap. They need to see action or they are uncomfortable with the client's emotional pain. These helpers often intervene prematurely with a prescribed course of action or quickly promote some step proposed by the client, when the client is not yet clear as to what the problem is.

The ideal client would go through a process like this:

1. They would quickly get to trust the helper. Talking to the helper and getting support would result in a lot of emotional stability.

2. They would talk over their problem a couple of times with you and would soon be clear on what the problem is.

3. They would see which parts of the problem are theirs and which belong to others.

4. Now they would be able to tell you clearly what the problem is and how they intend to free themselves from those parts which belong to others.
5. They would set a goal for themselves, i.e. the solution they desire.
6. They would set priorities for the steps they plan to take.
7. They would then begin working on the first winnable step.

Part of knowing when to help the client is being able to make an accurate assessment about the client's emotional stability and about their problem-solving skills.

Every bit as important is the information you get back from the client as you observe them taking on responsibility for helping themselves.

Timing interventions

Focus

This section aims to help you:
- develop skills in knowing when to help the client in setting goals and taking steps towards achieving those goals
- develop skills in testing the client's ability to take action steps now
- identify how to help the client to set their own time schedule for achieving their goals.

Illustrations

A. You are feeling stuck with Jean, a 45-year-old woman who came to you two months ago 'feeling very low'. Jean looks better and is much brighter. However, she does nothing but complain to you about the same old problem of not having any social life. You are getting tired of her complaining and are wondering how to get her moving.

B. Jack is a very anxious workaholic who has been making some mistakes at work. What really got to him a few weeks ago is that his in-laws want him and his wife Joyce to buy their house. Joyce has always wanted to live in her own house with a garden rather than in a rented flat. Joyce's parents want to move in to the house with them. Jack has been unable to make decisions lately. He cannot discuss it with his wife because of his high level of anxiety about the whole problem. Her parents are saying that they will wait another month for a decision.

Comments

In illustration A, the timing problem arises because the client, who has overcome her depressed feelings, is still going round in circles. The helper does not know what to do next.

In illustration B, there are external pressures of a deadline while the client is still in considerable emotional turmoil. The deadline may serve to increase the emotional storm. Do you wait until the client settles down or do you begin to challenge the client to take action steps towards resolving the problem?

Step by step procedure

1. Learn and practise the problem-solving procedures listed above in the portrait of the ideal client by applying them to your own problems.

2. Test the client's ability to take some achievable action steps. Check to see if the client is aware of simple things such as time of day, day of week, etc. Note how good the client's memory is, how well they keep appointments, etc. Note whether you feel easier inside when you are with the client. Does it feel more like a normal meeting now? These are just a few of the practical ways to test whether or not the client is ready to be nudged into action.

3. If the client is quite helpless you may have to do one of the steps for them. However, in doing this you will probably increase their dependence on you and you will get in the way of them helping themselves. Doing it for them will also deprive the client of good feelings about themselves.

4. Go over a time schedule with the client. Establish a framework for their schedule by writing in fixed times set by someone else, such as the family coming for Christmas, etc. If your client is pregnant, the baby will not wait twelve months to be born. Encourage your client to set their own time goals.

5. Let the client know that you expect reports of progress to you at appropriate points. Even if they take no action, they should still report.

6. Communicate to the client that together you will want to evaluate the whole experience as they proceed with the resolution of the problem.

7. Some helpers trained in listening skills sometimes get stuck because they do not know what to do as a next step. If your client week after week, keeps complaining or just sharing feelings, both of you may be stuck. It is time for the helper to get some supervision and to do some self-evaluation.

Bridging
The comments and procedures in this section apply to teaching situations where goals are involved, e.g. planning for retirement, for a change of a career, for a holiday or for a change of lifestyle.

Warning
- The most common trap the helper gets into with regard to timing is one of prematurely pushing the client to work on what the helper thinks would be a good solution.
- You should not expect from the client more than they are capable of doing and coping with.

Helping the client develop inner resources

Focus

In this section you will:
- learn how to assist your client in doing an inventory of their resources
- learn how to encourage your client to develop new inner resources necessary for coping with life.

Illustration

Jim has worked with a company for 15 years. He is a machinist and was recently promoted to foreman. He has lots of skills, but has always been shy and apologetic about himself. Since his promotion, he has become depressed and if he doesn't improve, he will be demoted to his old position. His superior believes in him and has suggested that he call you for help. You have had three meetings with him and talking has helped lessen his depressed feelings. You sense that this is not enough for Jim, that there is something more he and you can do about the problem. Jim needs you to help him rediscover his own inner resources, so he can make better use of them.

Comments

People who have been criticised a lot as children or who have had a series of failures, usually have difficulty in believing in themselves and often feel inadequate.

Such a feeling of inadequacy can lead to two extreme behaviour patterns. One is to take no risk or initiatives in solving the problems. The other extreme is to react to their feelings of inadequacy by taking on tasks that are beyond their ability in an effort to prove themselves.

Crucial to breaking one's negative pattern is making an accurate inventory of inner resources and weaknesses. Rather than have someone else do the inventory for us, it is far more acceptable if we do it for ourselves.

People under extreme stress as well as those who have very low opinions of themselves are often unable to believe that they have strength and inner resources. Part of the task in helping these people do an inventory is encouraging them to recognise and claim their strengths.

Any accurate inventory of inner strength will also include the identification of weaknesses and shortcomings. In selecting which resources we wish to develop, it is important that we keep in mind the principle of choosing achievable, realistic goals.

Step by step procedure

1. Once you have achieved a relationship with the client, as you work together on problem clarification, focus on how much the client is failing to use available inner resources and to what extent needed resources are missing.

2. When you realise that the client has resources they are not using, confront the client with your observation, using only one obvious instance as an example. Do *not* offer a list of your observations.

3. Invite the client to join you in a bragging exercise. Ask them to tell you up to ten strengths they have, good things that might be useful in relation to their problem.

4. Once the client has come up with several strengths, repeat them back to the client. If you have some of those qualities, tell the client but keep *your* list short.

5. Encourage the client to think of others which they may have missed. Then feed back what you hear.

6. Ask the client to write down the resources they have identified.

7. Have the client tell you which resources they have been using and when they last used particular resources.

8. Together identify resources which would be helpful but are not on the list.

9. Explore with the client practical and realistic goals for acquiring a particular resource, e.g. a sense of humour, skills in decision-making, or the ability to confront problems.

Bridging

The comments and procedures in this section have been tried and found useful in the following situations:
- small groups of people who are wanting to improve their confidence and self-image
- people who tend to under-use their skills and resources
- pairs of friends or colleagues who want to help each other to greater awareness of their inner resources.

Warning

Clients who are dependent on others or those who do a lot of blaming, have difficulty with these steps. They tend to believe that others will solve their problems or that others are responsible for their problems and they do not really need to look at themselves. Sometimes it's a real fear that they will find nothing but shortcomings. These people will need your support, or perhaps even professional help to deal with their blocks.

Helping the client build up external resources

Focus

This section will help you to:
- recognise the importance of external support systems
- learn how to assist your clients in doing an inventory
- help the client to take steps in building up a support system.

Illustration

Mary works full time, has three teenagers, and her husband recently walked out on them. Her nearest relatives live three thousand miles away. Her marriage has been in poor shape for three years since they moved to a different town so they made no couple friends. Time spent on her job, housework and the children prevented her from making her own friends.

Mary is literally in a panic now and hardly able to do her job. When she comes to you for help, all you know is that her husband has left and she has three teenagers. As she talked about her anxiety and pain, you picked up that you are about the only 'friend' she has to talk to; you are the only person giving her emotional support.

Comments

There is a good deal of evidence available today to indicate that loneliness and inadequate numbers of friends, relatives and neighbours are major causes of both physical and emotional illness.

A major task of every helper is to encourage and instruct the lonely and loners of our society in building support around them.

Research in America has shown that the larger the support system available to those in crisis, the sooner they come through it and the better they survive it.

Research on the West Coast of America has shown that the average healthy person has about 25 people in their support system, while the mentally ill person has only about seven.

Step by step procedure

1. Prepare an inventory of your own support system, in order to understand the importance of a support system for your client. How many people would be available to you for support or companionship during a crisis? Is your system adequate?

2. Assuming you know your client a little, you are ready to help them look at their support system. Tell your client your observations, not opinions, of their support system.

3. Ask the client to make a list of the people who are in their support system. Request that they make some notes of the availability of each person.

4. If the client is not using people who are available, not reaching out and asking for support, point this out. Be firm, confronting and supportive, but do not accept excuses.

5. Encourage the client to select a few people and to begin asking for support and companionship.

6. Get the client to:
   - make a list of places to go to meet people, and
   - to note how they might begin building up a support system. Do not offer your suggestions until you have evidence that the client is actually working and producing their own list and notes.

7. Encourage the client to take some first achievable steps on their own and to report back to you.

8. It is important to get the client to set a date to report back to you on any actions they have agreed to take towards any of the above steps.

9. As the client develops more external resources, they will need you less, as they will look after their emotional needs in the normal ways used by average people day by day.

Bridging

The material in this chapter can be used with people who have recently moved to a new area. It can be used with people whose children are about to leave home. Or it can be used in preparation for retirement.

Warning

A few individuals have had little or no experience in social situations. Their skills are few and far between. Some others are really afraid of closeness. Do not give up on these slow starters; simply use good sense in nudging them into action, remembering that their own pace may be somewhat different from yours.

Motivating the resistant client

Focus

In this section you will:
- learn ways to use the client's resistance rather than getting stuck or giving up
- discover the importance of using the client's resistance as a way of helping them to help themselves
- learn ways to identify your own response to the client's resistance.

Illustration

Irma is 45 years old, lives alone and has worked for her company as a secretary for 20 years. She has always tended to get attention by complaining about a lot of little things. Her complaining increased about six months ago after her mother died. The other people in her department decided to 'gang up' on her, being tired of her complaining. Irma came to you and after six or seven meetings had stopped a lot of the complaining. She began to see that she needed attention and affection. You were expecting that she would start doing something by way of making friends and getting out.

However, Irma has become anxious about moving to a new house and has started complaining again. She is now complaining to you that the counselling isn't helping her. Unless you talk about this resistance, she could simply leave and not return, missing the opportunity to improve her life.

Comments

Resistance is used by the client as a way of blocking progress or change. Frequently the client is unaware of blocking or, if aware, has some rational explanation about what is happening.

The blocking can take the form of stubborn silence, changing the topic, forgetting appointments, getting into some new kind of trouble or reverting back to old patterns (which had disappeared).

Generally, resistance is a means used by the client to regain some measure of comfort or control, in the face of fear: the fear of getting too close to strong feelings or the fear of change. As ineffective, destructive, maybe even painful, as old patterns of coping may be for the client, there is some comfort in maintaining them; it may be all the client knows!

Responding to the client with anger and frustration only makes matters worse and both get stuck in the confrontation. What will work though is an approach which has two clearly related steps.

The *first* step is to become aware of and respond to the fear behind the resistance. For help in doing this refer back to the chapter on listening to and responding to feelings. For example, you can respond to the non-verbal clues provided by the client who has stopped talking and gives you only silence.

The *second* step is to talk about the fear behind the resistance. Once the client knows that you understand and care, they may be able to consider and talk about their feelings. Then later you will be able to point out to the client how they were using resistance behaviour in an honest effort to protect against the feared pain and discomfort.

Step by step procedure

1. When faced with resistance reflect on your own feelings.

2. Review what you know about the client to get some picture of what fear and other feelings may be behind the resistance.

3. If you sense that the client is of a very anti-social type, check this with a professional. Anti-social personalities are usually very clever and cunning. You will find it impossible to work with the resistance they give. These people have little interest in responding to or in improving through counselling or therapy.

4. Begin listening and responding to the feelings and fear behind the resistance.

5. After the feelings are acceptable to the client and the fear has eased, begin to explore together. Point out to the client what you observed in the resistant behaviour without passing judgment. Invite the client to explore with you what it is all about.

6. Together you can now move back to wherever you were in identifying or resolving the problem. *You will both have learned from the interruption.*

7. Evaluate your own responses to the resistance. Explore whether or not you took the resistance personally, and how you were different as a helper when you understood the resistance as part of the client's struggle.

8. Take some time to reflect on resistance in the client as an opportunity for working together towards the client's health and resolving their problems.

Bridging

What you discover in this session may also apply to certain systems, like families, groups or departments. This section does not apply to the unwilling client who has been sent and simply does not want to be there. It applies to those situations where the client has expressed interest in changing for the better. The group or client may want change but is afraid of it and does not want to give up 'the way I/we used to do it'.

Warning

Beware of 'banging your head against a brick wall' with those clients whose lifestyle is close to total manipulation of others. Anti-social personalities are of this type. Alcoholics who are not doing anything about a cure either through AA or elsewhere, will not work with you on their resistance.

Learning how to evaluate

Focus

In this section you will:
- learn that in assisting the client to evaluate you are contributing to their future mental health
- learn effective evaluation skills.

Illustration

Hazel and you have had five meetings together. She is a single parent with three boys. The boys are aged 11 to 15. She came to you in a panic two days after her 15-year-old got caught at school sharing out some drugs with four of his friends. She was unable to go to work the first day because she was beside herself. Once she cooled down she made a number of creative changes in relation to her children and her ex-husband who lives in a nearby town. There are problems still with her son at school, and it will be seven years before the youngest son has finished school. In the previous meeting Hazel got angry with you because she thought that you were criticising her parental role.

Comments

Evaluation in the helping process has three important functions.
- It helps you to learn from the experience.
- Evaluation can be a help in getting unstuck when there is a problem issue in the helping relationship as in the above example.
- Evaluation has the effect of providing some sense of direction. 'If you are going to know where you are going you have to know where you have been.'

We would differentiate between this kind of evaluation and the problem clarification described in Part 2, p. 86. What is of interest is the experience the client is having as they share with you and work on resolving the problem. The client may be helped to evaluate the steps they are taking towards resolving the problem. Together you may evaluate the experience you have had and are still having in the helping relationship.

A most important goal in all helping, except in continuing supportive relationships with some emotionally handicapped people, is to arrive at the time when the client no longer needs you. In the next section, I will touch on evaluation as part of the process of ending a helping relationship.

Step by step procedure

1. Early in establishing the helping relationship let the client know that you expect to do some evaluation together along the way.

2. Introduce the first experience of evaluation at the close of the first meeting with something like, 'Let's talk for a minute or two about how you feel this meeting has gone'. If it seems important, end every meeting in a similar manner.

3. Whenever the client reports some success in something they have done about the problem, take time before the end of the session to get them to talk about their contribution to the success. Do the same with disappointments and perceived failures. Be careful not to be judgmental.

4. Whenever you feel that you and the client have reached a flat plateau, going nowhere, introduce evaluation as a way of getting things going again. This may lead to a referral or to terminating your meetings.

5. Introduce and use evaluation as a way of testing whether it is appropriate to begin ending the helping relationship.

6. If one of your helping goals is to aid the client in gaining improved mental health and ability to cope with life without you, then you must introduce evaluation as a major part of the termination (ending session) you have together.

Bridging

The material in this session overlaps with the section on referrals and endings (pp. 31 and 104). It can be used in working with groups or with committees, or in a great variety of teamwork situations.

Warning

If you do the evaluation work of the client, then you may not only deprive the client of an opportunity to 'grow', but you may damage the helping relationship.

Successfully ending a helping relationship

Focus

This section will help you consider:
- when ending is appropriate
- the importance of dealing with endings
- appropriate 'goodbyes'.

Illustration

You are meeting Sue for the third time. You were expecting that she might bring up the question of terminating your meetings together. As she was leaving the previous session, she mentioned having seen you and her supervisor together at lunch.

At the beginning of this session she announces that she doesn't need your help any more. Yet Sue had very serious problems two weeks ago. Is this ending appropriate? How do you find out?

Comments

People tend to end helping relationships using the same patterns they use when they end other relationships.
- Some people tend to end relationships prematurely.
- Others leave without saying goodbye.
- Some actually leave but hang on to the relationship emotionally (often with destructive results).

The death of a close friend or of a family member is a traumatic ending. So is losing the ability to play sport through a permanent injury.

All the little and medium endings in life serve as important preparation for the more traumatic endings. The experience in the little endings helps to set the pattern for how to cope with the unexpected and often tragic endings.

The experience the client has of ending with the helper is an opportunity to develop a new ability to cope with other 'endings' in the future. Many people who experience emotional difficulties have had unhappy endings in the past and may have developed a pattern of avoiding the feelings that go with endings or may even avoid the ending itself and just not turn up any more; no reasons given. There are helpers who out of their own tendency to avoid endings, aid and abet the client in the avoidance. It becomes important therefore, for the helper to understand their own feelings about endings. Read the section on losses and endings in Chapter V (p. 111).

Knowing when ending is appropriate is a skill which comes from experience. Premature endings may be initiated by the client for one of the following reasons:
- The client knows the helper will sooner or later introduce the question of ending so the client leaves first as a way of avoiding the hurt.
- Some type of tension, discomfort or misunderstanding has emerged in the helping relationship.
- The counselling got too close to some fearful feeling or issue.

Evaluation is part of any creative ending. The helper may remind the client of the goals you agreed to work on. However the client needs to do most of the evaluation. With your encouragement the client can tell you:

- how well the goals were reached
- what disappointments were experienced
- what the overall experience was like
- what tasks remain for the client to work on
- what they expect it will be like without the regular meetings.

You can bring fairness and reality to the ending by sharing your own satisfactions, disappointments and feelings about the ending. However, helpers need to be careful not to do the client's work at this point.

Appropriate final goodbyes involve being clear that this is the last meeting and acknowledging any 'dragging of the feet' in saying goodbye. A handshake, an embrace, whichever seems appropriate and then walking away, closing the door or some clear symbol that this is the end.

Step by step procedure

1. Listen for verbal clues and watch for non-verbal clues which may indicate a premature ending.

2. If the helping relationship is being prolonged beyond what is necessary, talk to yourself or better still, to a colleague or supervisor.

3. With either step 1 or 2 completed, it's now time to talk to your client about what is happening in the helping relationship. In any case, attempt to get to the feelings or concerns behind the behaviour.

4. If the client is upset by the notion of ending your sessions, reassure them. Tell them that it will be better to remain and to move ahead at a comfortable pace rather than to stop with things unresolved.

5. If the imminent ending is because of a problem between you, assure the client that you really care about knowing what it is and that you can work together to resolve the matter.

6. When both the client and helper agree that ending is appropriate, then it's time to set up a procedure for evaluating and saying goodbye.

7. Now do the evaluation together:
    - State the original goals.
    - Set the client to list the goals reached, together with any disappointments.

8. Encourage the client to continue helping themselves with any unfinished business.

9. Then say goodbye in whatever way is appropriate, making sure it is clear and final.

10. In situations where you work together or where social activities will bring you together, it is important to end the 'helping' relationship as such. This should leave you both clear about the difference between the two kinds of relationships.

Bridging

The principles and skills outlined here would apply to ending those relationships where there has been some type of contract, or agreement. The focus in all situations should be evaluating goals worked on, bringing to the surface feelings related to endings and acceptance of the end of the relationship.

Warning

Clients who have difficulty with endings are quick to sense whether the helper has difficulty too. Learning skills in how to help the client get the most out of endings will be of no help without some real self-insight by you in how you handle endings and losses.

CHAPTER V
SPECIAL SITUATIONS

Introduction

This chapter covers special situations. Developing skills in these situations will make things a lot easier for you when faced with them.

One section focuses on the most important skill of them all; the skill of being able to keep confidential everything your client shares with you.

This chapter provides materials covering the following situations:
- post emergency follow-up
- client's responses to losses
- support for the emotionally handicapped
- working with the alcoholic
- HIV counselling
- helping somebody who is antibody positive
- intervention in suicide situations
- working with the depressed person
- facing possible terminal illness
- marital and family break-up
- teenage run-aways
- confidentiality
- the helper gets help.

A short list of resources

The availability of resources depends on a number of factors:
- *Rural* or *large city*
- *Remoteness* from the centres
- *Affluence* of the community. Often the middle class has the least resources for emotional emergencies.

How to go about finding the resource you need for making referrals depends in part on where you live and in part on where to turn to ask for information about available resources. Simply because a professional doesn't know about a particular resource does not mean that it's not there.

The list below focuses on where to turn for information about what's available.

Where to go in rural areas

Minister or priest	Medical doctor
Hospital chaplain	Samaritans
Social services	Hospital social worker
Citizen Advice Bureaux	Any self-help group
Ex-social worker	Womens' Institute

Where to go in the small town

Samaritans	Medical doctor
Minister or priest	Headmaster/Headmistress
Psychiatrist	Psychologist
The social services	
The hospital [look for chaplain or social worker]	

The older small town usually has a network of informal information services and groups which works quite well.

The newer growing towns are often without adequate resources. Furthermore, those people who are providing services often do not know who else is providing services.

Where to go in the large cities and suburbs

The most obvious sources of information are:
1. The local paper
2. Churches
3. Community centres
4. Yellow Pages
5. Thompsons Local Directories
6. Social security offices.

Post emergency follow-up

Focus

This section provides you with:
- a checklist for you to use in making certain that you provide adequate follow-up.
- help in determining when follow-up is important.

Illustration

You were the helper who responded to the call for help from Helena's husband. Helena was cracking up as she waited for surgery on a lump under her arm. You not only listened to her concerns, but you supported her in going to see her doctor that same day to get information about some of her unanswered questions. The emergency ended after her talk with the doctor.

Comments

In the illustration above, several questions should be considered by the helper now that the emergency is over.
- Will Helena get herself into another emergency before the operation?
- If no emergency develops, could Helena benefit from a few more opportunities to talk with you before the operation?
- In view of her reluctance to talk over private matters and to ask for support, how do you approach her so that she does not turn down your offer?
- How will things be for Helena after the surgery and after she comes home from the hospital?
- What about an evaluation together of the whole helping experience which you both share? Might this be a way of Helena learning to be more open with people in her support system when she gets worried?

Those people who have come through a crisis in life and are more able than ever before to handle future crises will have:
- had an adequate support system, both in terms of numbers and of competence
- had support when they needed it
- evaluated the experience and learned from it.

Having support when they need it includes having support during the post emergency period. If you are the helper who provides that support, then you should know:
- when *not* to terminate the relationship
- when to intervene once the professional has finished
- when to get out of the picture and not be in the way of the client helping themselves
- how to help the client evaluate the experience and so to contribute to valuable learning of new skills for both the client and yourself.

Step by step procedure

1. Determine whether the emergency is over. Use the section on knowing when it's an emergency for your guidelines, p. 28.

2. If it's over, check the following and select those steps which are important for this particular situation:
   - Are professionals available as needed?
   - Does the client need continuing, non-professional support to prevent another emergency happening soon?
   - Is there likely to be a critical time in the days or weeks ahead as things work out? When will it be critical?
   - Who will be available for continuing support and/or for the critical time(s)?
   - Has the client evaluated the experience so that they can be stronger next time?
   - When would be the best time to evaluate?
   - Are you willing to be involved as necessary and appropriate?

3. Do those things that are necessary providing you are willing, available and capable.

4. Be firm and tactful when the client resists help. See p. 100.

5. Support the client in getting some other helper if you cannot do the important tasks.

6. End the relationship in a helpful way. See p. 104, *Successfully ending a helping relationship*.

Bridging
The following sections will be valuable in doing post emergency follow-up:
- all of Chapter IV, Part 1
- all of Chapter IV, Part 3 with special emphasis on the last two sections.

Warning
During post emergency follow-up, you must be clear about your role as distinct from the responsibilities of any professionals involved. You should be supporting the prescriptions given by the professionals.

The client's responses to endings and losses

Focus

This section will help you to:
- appreciate the importance of helping clients to face losses and work through grief
- learn how to get to the feelings generated by endings in both helper and client.
- motivate the client to take responsibility for letting go.

Illustrations

A. You have been providing supportive counselling for Maude who has been living in the same place for 20 years. She was severely upset five years ago for a period after the death of her only child. You get together once a month, mostly to talk about her ability to cope in her job and how she feels about herself. She is doing well and really doesn't need the support any longer. Others need your time more.

B. Arthur was in a severe accident four years ago. He had some brain damage but does well at his job as a book-keeper, except that he gets confused when under a lot of stress. You are available to him for a chat when he needs you. He became very upset when he discovered that you will be leaving and moving to another area in four months.

Comments

In illustration A, Maude, like a lot of emotionally troubled people, found herself unable to cope with common crises in her life because of earlier big losses. Her mother died when she was four, that was the first big loss. She used to get depressed every time she moved. Years later her only child was killed in an accident.

Many people whom we help have difficulty with losses and endings. When the helping relationship ends they can
- continue to grow in strength, or
- be no stronger or able to cope than when they started, or
- be much less able to handle future crises.

It is fairly common in helping situations for things to deteriorate after the idea of ending has surfaced, whether it was brought up by the helper or the client. It is also common for everyone involved to avoid the feelings generated by the idea of ending. This avoidance can be the real cause of the deterioration and setback.

Sometimes these clients will create a new problem as a way of avoiding ending the relationship. Helpers also have been known to hang on to their clients, reasoning that the client still needs help. Whatever patterns emerge at ending time, it is safe to assume that the client may have slipped back to well-used, but ineffective ways of handling losses.

The skilful helper can help the client to work it out this time by using the ending as a valuable learning experience. However, that will not happen if both the helper and the client ignore and avoid the feelings generated by the loss.

It is important to create opportunities to evaluate as outlined on p. 102. The helper needs to be aware of
- feelings about the ending itself
- possible anger at the helper, mixed with affection and gratitude
- anxiety about making it on their own without the helper
- avoidance of the feelings by not saying 'goodbye' and attempting to set up some vague arrangement for the future. Note how often people say 'I'll be seeing you' when there is little likelihood of that happening within any reasonable time, if ever.

Confrontation skills outlined in earlier chapters will aid the helper in bringing these issues to the surface where the client can learn and experience more creative ways of facing endings and losses.

Step by step procedure

1. Reflect on how you as a person usually handle endings. If you sense that you have blind spots, talk to another helper about how you experience endings.

2. When the issue of ending comes up, remember who initiated the matter and in what circumstances. You will be able to use this information later in your client's own interest.

3. When it's clear that the client has accepted and acknowledged that the ending will take place, communicate clearly to the client that you will want to
   - talk over what you have done together
   - explore what the client may wish to do after ending, in terms of helping themselves and
   - that you will want to share together how each of you experiences and feels about the termination of the relationship.

4. If your client agrees to the above, then you take responsibility for seeing that there is plenty of opportunity to evaluate, explore and share feelings about this and other losses.

5. If you are actually ending, follow the steps on p. 102 regarding evaluating with the client.

6. To learn by talking about losses and endings, you need to get to the feelings. You can do this by responding to feelings expressed verbally or non-verbally, or initiating something like, 'We all have feelings about losses and endings; let's talk about how we both feel about the possible end of this relationship.'

7. Encourage the client to compare these feelings with how they managed losses in the past.

8. When it comes to the last meeting, follow the procedures on p. 104 and you will both have profited by facing and accepting the reality of the loss.

Bridging

The material in this session applies to most situations in life where endings and feelings of loss are involved. It could be:
- someone leaving or transferring from their job
- the break-up of a marriage or some other relationship
- death, either at work or in your private life.

Warning

The step by step procedures above will not be useful where your relationship with the client has been brief and no real relationship has developed.

Supportive counselling for the emotionally handicapped

Focus

This section can be used to learn about the importance of supportive counselling.

Illustration

Bill developed epileptic attacks when he was 12. It took about four years of medical research and care before his attacks stopped completely. He is still on medication. He has a job, but he has no social skills and appears to have suffered some permanent emotional damage. A major problem is finding a living situation for him where he will get some emotional support and some guidance. He needs support in order to maintain what self-confidence he has.

Comments

Many of us at some point in life develop a handicap. If we have difficulty in seeing clearly at distances, we learned to wear glasses to drive a car, or to watch a film. We learned to accept our dependency on glasses in those situations.

Likewise there are people who are emotionally handicapped and who need continuing support. They do not need 'emotional first aid' so much as adequate support systems. It is not the advanced training of the supportive helper that counts; it is the quality of the supportive relationship. A creative relationship will make all the difference to how well these people cope with everyday life in general.

Just as important to their coping is the extent to which they are permitted and encouraged to lead normal lives at work, at home and out in the community. For a lot of these people some of the modern medications have made the difference between institutional care and living in the community. The medication does not create health. The medication tends to relieve the emotional turmoil to the extent that the person in conjunction with their support system creates their own health and ability to cope.

Identifying the emotionally handicapped

It is not up to you or to me to determine on our own that an individual is emotionally handicapped on a permanent basis. Such an evaluation should be done by people who know what they are doing and should always include a number of such professionals. The section of making referrals, p. 31, will help you get such assistance. There are individuals who need to be evaluated by a psychiatrist before you or I make any commitment to helping them. Any report from a person in the mental health professions should be taken seriously.

With increased community acceptance, people who have handicaps or who are very dependent on medication tend to talk freely about their handicap. If you suspect that an individual is on medication or is in the care of a mental health professional, it is important that you ask direct questions about the medication and who it is they are seeing.

Society, including the government, believes that people attain a greater measure of health when they live in the community rather than in mental health institutions, and that it is less costly in financial terms.

Look back at the section in Chapter III on what to do when a client needs a psychiatrist or similar medical attention, p. 33. Remember, at this point, you are learning about supportive counselling for the emotionally handicapped. Supportive counselling has many benefits.

For this to be effective, there are some specific things to learn and to watch for which I will outline in the step by step procedures.

Step by step procedure

1. Check your tolerance for having clients dependent on you. Helpers who take on too many dependent clients will reach exhaustion level more quickly than if they are working with people who are able to help themselves.

2. Try and gain some insight into your own patterns in working with dependent people. For example, do you tend to give too much and then silently resent what you are doing?

3. Set limits on the number of emotionally handicapped people you will see in proportion to your total number of clients.

4. Watch your expectations when working with the emotionally handicapped. You take responsibility away from the client when you do too much and expect too little. On the other hand, you set both yourself and the client up for failure when you expect too much of the client.

5. Know your role concerning the client's medication. You are not a doctor and you have no business trying to be a medical person. However, you have a very important role with the emotionally handicapped who are on medication. Often these people have either forgotten the original directions from their doctor, or they did not understand in the first place Some of them may even have decided to be their own doctors and have either stopped or increased the dosage. Some have been influenced by well-meaning relatives or friends.

    Your role is to encourage the client to stay with the doctor's instructions and prescriptions. If you have any reason to believe that the client has misunderstood, is fooling around with the medication or has stopped it altogether, tell the client you want them to talk to the doctor as soon as possible.

6. If you have any doubts or misgivings about the prescribed medication, do not communicate your doubts to the client. Instead simply tell your client that as a matter of procedure, you are requesting that they review the medication with a physician, or with a specialist.

7. Exercise your responsibility to encourage all your clients, particularly those who are emotionally handicapped, to maintain a good-sized support system. If it's too small, push them to build a larger one. Do *not* accept the client's resistance to doing something about it. Dependent clients have a way of seducing helpers into thinking that they alone 'understand'.

    Keep in mind that most communities have competent and often trained volunteers who can be useful to the emotionally handicapped.

8. Make sure that you get to know some of the other people in your client's support system. Insist on getting the client's permission to consult with a few of these people. Consult with doctors, AA sponsors, etc. Beware of consulting behind the client's back without their knowledge of the nature of the consultation.

9. This would be a good point to read the section on confidentiality, p. 139.

Bridging

The step by step procedures above apply to many situations where there is a physical handicap whether or not there is an emotional handicap.

Warning

- Remember, even with people who need to depend on you, the principle of helping people to help themselves is still extremely important.
- Watch for your own negative feelings about particular emotional handicaps. Let someone else provide the support in those situations. Later, you may do something about resolving those negative feelings.

Working with the alcoholic

Focus

This section will help you:
- improve your understanding of the defence patterns used by the alcoholic client.
- develop skills that will enable you to attain a higher level of success when counselling the alcoholic
- improve your skills in utilising other support for the client, e.g. Alcoholics Anonymous.

Illustration

Jim has been a heavy drinker for years. Until recently, it showed in his work only on Mondays, the result of heavy week-end drinking. For the past three months he has been drinking every day. This change came about straight after his father died. He smells of alcohol and is a bit unsteady when he comes to talk with you.

Comments

Alcoholism is not only a widespread problem in our society, it is one of the most difficult for both professionals and helpers to work with. Several patterns used by the average alcoholic make things difficult for the helper:
- Alcoholics use denial as a way of avoiding their problem(s).
- There is usually an internal conflict over the child-like need to be dependent. Alcoholics fight this by being extremely independent (counter-dependent).
- Alcoholics often act out strong feelings of guilt.
- Perhaps, most difficult for the helper, is the manipulation used by alcoholics. They will play on your sympathy or use some other method to 'make you part of their problem' rather than change themselves.

There is a widespread belief in our society that alcoholics have to reach 'rock-bottom' before they can be helped. Yet there are many opportunities to help alcoholics to help themselves with related or underlying problems before bottom is reached. The Catch-22 in working with the alcoholic is that it is futile to work on the emotions and the underlying problems unless the client stops drinking. If you get involved in 'drying them out', you will never get to work together on either the emotions or the other problems.

I have worked out a model of working with alcoholics that results in a high success rate. I offer to establish a helping relationship with the alcoholic to work together on the emotions and other problems, *only* if the client makes a *commitment* to:
- seek regular help from Alcoholics Anonymous
- agree to a contract where I can check the commitment and, if I find the client is not keeping the commitment, I will terminate the counselling. Basically, this results in the client remaining sober or having to deal with 'slips' elsewhere and we are free to focus on our counselling goals.

One difficulty helpers encounter is with the client who is a borderline alcoholic and who denies that there is a drinking problem. The helper needs clear definitions of alcoholism and objective sources of information in order to make a decision about whether or not to apply the above ground-rules.

You can use the AA definition as one measure. Contact your local AA for their checklist. The medical definition divides alcoholism into three categories:

1. Alcoholic addiction.
2. Episodic excessive drinking.
3. Habitual excessive drinking.

With information from sources other than the client, together with your observations, it is not so difficult to identify the alcoholic client. If there has been excessive, habitual drinking for a continuous period of at least three months, simply tell that client that you will not work with them unless one of the above requirements listed above is met.

Treat 'binge drinking' differently. Request that they not come to an appointment if they have been drinking during the previous 24 hours.

Apply the more rigid requirements to the habitual, excessive-drinking client. More time is needed to gather the information in order to distinguish between this category and the binge drinker. A good yardstick is the medical definition: 'An alcoholic is someone who is obviously under the influence more than once a week or who is intoxicated more than twelve times yearly'.

In gathering the information and in the subsequent agreeing of ground-rules, the helper must be firm, gentle and caring with the client, all at the same time.

Step by step procedure

1. If you know there is drinking, face the client with that awareness early in the first meeting.

2. Before the first meeting ends, make it clear to the client that you are interested in helpingwith their problems, but that you will not take on the task of helping them control any drinking problem.

3. Gather as much information as you can about the client's drinking patterns and the amount of drinking. Tell the client that it is important for you to know this about them in order to help with the other problems.

4. Also in the first meeting, ask the client for permission to talk to people about the drinking patterns. If the client refuses, inform them that you cannot help without full and accurate information. Do not allow yourself to be manipulated at this point.

5. If you are certain, by the end of the first meeting, that the client is an alcoholic or an excessive habitual drinker, request that before the next meeting they provide you with the name of their AA sponsor.

6. Make sure that you talk to that other helper before you agree to any long-term counselling with the client. Usually these other helpers are glad to learn about your role with the client. The AA sponsor will be open to meeting with you and the client to clarify your roles.

7. Stay clear about your role with the client. As you spell out the role and your goals, make it clear again that you do not wish to get involved in whether the client drinks or not, that it is between the client and the other helper. However, be firm about the client maintaining a regular relationship with the other helper.

8. If and when the client drinks, accept it and tell the client to work through the bad feelings with the other helper. Do not accept any termination of the relationship with the other helper.

9. Work at not getting caught in the client's problems of dependent needs. With this approach, the client is caught in a Catch-22 situation. The client has to take steps to end the drinking problem or they lose the one helping relationship where the concern is about emotions and life's problems, and where drinking does not become an issue.

Bridging
Many of the principles and suggestions in this chapter apply to a person addicted to either illegal or prescribed drugs. A number of alcoholics are already on drugs while others change to drug addiction when they stop drinking.

Warning
Be aware of any tendency on your part to think that you can get the alcoholic to stop drinking. Furthermore, watch out for distorted expectations you may have of your being able to help the alcoholic client while they continue excessive alcoholic drinking.

HIV pre- and post-test counselling

Focus

In this section you will cover the main aspects of pre- and post-test counselling.

Illustration

A. Stephanie has just ended an affair with a bisexual man who has told her he has the AIDS virus. She is beside herself with fear and finds herself unable to concentrate on her job as a teacher at a local infants school. Apart from her fears for herself, she is also afraid of infecting the children. In addition, she has just started going out with a man she likes very much, and who has expressed strong feelings and a commitment towards her.

B. Bert discovered recently that the man he shared rooms with at College was gay. Bert has subsequently been feeling rather poorly, with aching limbs, swollen feet, chest pains, strange rashes all over his body (which irritatingly disappear whenever he goes for a medical consultation). He is still a virgin, but he is convinced that he has AIDS, as a result of sharing a room with this man. His GP has given him three HIV antibody tests, and has refused to give him any more. Bert has approached you in the hope that you will understand and arrange his fourth blood test.

Comments

The blood test for HIV detects antibodies to the virus: it is not a direct test for the virus itself, and is not a test for AIDS. It does not predict who will go on to develop the symptoms. So, individuals may go for many years carrying antibodies to the virus without developing symptoms to it. On the other hand, where the virus is active, its effect comes from the destruction of vital white cells in the blood which work to kill off the various bacteria and viruses which attack the body. Consequently conditions arise as a result of the host's immune deficiency which can no longer keep these micro-organisms in check. These disease processes are known as 'opportunistic conditions', because they arise from the opportunity offered by an immune-incompetent host.

HIV is not fussy: it does not respect geographic, economic, ethnic, age or political boundaries. Neither is it predictable in terms of its mode or timing or symptom expression.

The functioning of pre-test counselling is:
- to portray the options and outcome regarding a positive result
- to determine what the client understands about the HIV antibody test, and correct misconceptions
- to assess whether the client has a realistic expectation of a positive result
- to go over necessary changes in lifestyle irrespective of the result: safer sex, and safer drug-taking to avoid exposing oneself or others to HIV
- to establish what are the advantages and disadvantages of having the test.

At the end of the pre-test counselling session, the client should be able to make an informed decision as to whether or not to go ahead with the test.

The pre-test counselling also allows the opportunity to pick up whether or not the request is appropriate, and then to redirect the client to appropriate help as necessary. For example, an individual requesting his fourth HIV antibody test in the absence of any intervening sexual activity, is clearly not going to be helped by another test. It is then a question of referring on.

The aim of the post-test counselling session is to interpret what being HIV antibody positive means for the individual client:
- what changes are necessary in their life to adapt to having the virus
- who should they tell, and what should they tell.

You will have to:
- reiterate what the antibody test result means
- explain infection control procedures
- reassure them about the safety of casual social contact
- arrange a follow up appointment.

The follow-up appointment is vital in order to review information which may not have got through on the first occasion, and to give the opportunity for the client to ask questions which they will have thought of during the intervening period.

Make sure you know the reason behind any referral of a client to you. If it is for information-giving, include reference to leaflets and so on in the session. If it is about the uncertainty of whether or not to have the HIV antibody test, then you can refer the client to the appropriate counselling facility attached to a district hospital's Sexually Transmittable Disease clinic. If this is not possible, and there is no other trained individual available to do it, raise the issues yourself, provided you are prepared and able to follow them through until a referral on can be made.

Step by step procedure

1. Establish the client's degree of risk of exposure to HIV, as a means of gauging how they might react to a positive result, and as a means of filtering out individuals with hypo-chondriac tendencies – i.e. people who go for more than one test, following a negative result, and in the absence of any risk of exposure to HIV.

2. Discuss disadvantages at this stage. For example:
   - the difficulties in obtaining life insurance
   - the stress of coping with a positive result
   - the possibility that employers and others will find out about the result and the subsequent possibility of being rejected.

3. Present possible advantages. For example:
   - the need to protect current sexual partners
   - the implications with respect to family planning
   - the possibility that therapy or treatments (especially those discovered in the future) could benefit people carrying the virus who are otherwise well
   - the resolution of the uncertainty surrounding not knowing
   - for medical diagnostic purposes for individuals with symptoms of unknown origin.

4. Sound out whether or not the client has a realistic expectation of the test result either way, and if so encourage them to make a positive decision to have the test or not.

5. If the client elects to have the test, then ensure that they make an appointment to receive the results in person, irrespective of whether or not it is positive or negative.

6. Arrange with the individual who gives the result that the client receives full post-test counselling and follow-up.

Bridging

- This situation requires the basic counselling skills demonstrated throughout the book.
- The material also links in with that presented during the desensitisation exercise on p. 5.

Warning

It is absolutely essential that anyone who is considering having the test for antibodies to HIV receives pre-test counselling. If you come across any incidents where this has not happened you should draw it to the attention of the appropriate health service management, who should follow it up.

Helping somebody who is antibody positive

Focus

The purpose of this section is to:
- identify the main issues facing persons who are HIV antibody positive but who do not have the symptoms
- identify the main issues facing persons who have the symptoms of HIV.

Illustration A

Ted found out he was HIV antibody positive two weeks ago when he had a test at a private clinic. He had not had either pre- or post-test counselling. At the time he took the news in his stride: he was expecting a positive result, and he was in good health. Over the last few days however, he has begun to feel panicky. He feels he can no longer cope with his job as manager of a book shop, and he has uncharacteristically taken the last few days off sick.

Comments

There are a range of counselling needs facing individuals who are HIV antibody positive but without symptoms. Overall, the main concerns are related to:
- the uncertainty of not knowing whether or not symptoms will develop
- the social stigma attached to AIDS and the consequent experience of others' prejudices when individuals are identified publicly as antibody positive; related to this is the issue of who to tell, and what to tell them
- the fear of infecting others
- adjusting to changes in lifestyle as a result of being HIV antibody positive.

These points are by no means exhaustive, and simply represent common psychosocial themes seen in the context of individual reactions to HIV. The prerequisites for any individual or service offered to people in connection with HIV infection are:
- that they assure confidentiality
- present consistent information
- that they offer good access to the service.

> ### Step by step procedure
>
> 1. Be clear about what other care the patient is receiving and how you fit in with that. If some needs are not being met, use your knowledge of the local organisation set up to assist.
>
> 2. Establish what the patient knows about HIV, and their current physical condition. Check out with any available data. Clarify any inconsistencies and misunderstandings about HIV.
>
> 3. Reassure them of the safety of casual social contact, and the lack of risk posed for others living with someone who is HIV antibody positive. Instruct them in clearing up body-fluid spillages (one part bleach diluted to nine parts water is recommended).
>
> 4. Discuss who should be informed about the client's status, and caution against telling anyone without full consideration of the consequences. This applies especially to individuals who have recently discovered their antibody status.
>
> 5. In terms of uncertainty, clarify whether its effects are debilitating as a result of high levels of acute anxiety, and intervene or refer on accordingly. Beyond the symptomatic level, establish the source of the uncertainty and intervene appropriately. So, if it relates to lack of information or understanding, replace the ignorance and fear with facts as they are currently known. If it relates to basic fears about what HIV leads to, encourage the client to spell out these fears and to discuss them.
>
> 6. Offer basic health boosting advice and information about diet, exercise, moderate intake of alcohol, and about groups that help people stop smoking, and so on.

Illustration B

Martin should be admitted to hospital as a result of his increasing shortness of breath, possibly related to HIV infection. He is highly anxious and refuses to take up the bed which his doctor has organised. Neither work-mates nor family are aware of the fact that he is HIV antibody positive, and so he is unable to share his fears about what is going on. He has had a furious argument with his partner who has stormed off to cool down.

Comments

One of the main difficulties facing people when they develop symptoms to the virus is that it is often no longer possible for them to cover up that everything is all right. It may well be that they are broaching the subject of hospitalisation for the first time with themselves, their loved ones, and their colleagues at work.

Issues discussed in the previous section on the symptom-free phase apply equally here. There is so much uncertainty about whether symptoms will go into remission or get worse, whether there are any treatments available for the particular symptoms, and so on. The principal drug is AZT, but this cannot be tolerated by everybody, and it cannot actually reverse the underlying immune deficiency. On the other hand, there is evidence that it does prolong life.

Social prejudice abounds, and the client is in the position of being more exposed to it depending on how their symptoms manifest themselves.

Amongst a range of psychological phenomena there is the issue of health preoccupation: clients become acutely aware of daily variations in physical feelings and are primed to interpret these changes as emerging symptoms. Moreover, reactions to the diagnosis of being found HIV antibody positive can include high anxiety levels. The heightened level of arousal interferes with thinking, with concentration, memory, attending to the present and so on. Some clients with anxiety-related difficulties in thinking mistakenly attribute the problem to HIV in the central nervous system (HIV affects both the immune and the central nervous systems). They suspect they are suffering the AIDS dementia of which they have heard. In these cases it is important to rule out organic causes, and equally important to be aware of the psychological factors in order to intervene appropriately.

> ## Step by step procedure
>
> 1. Appraise your involvement with your client and how you fit in with others involved. If you are going to be involved in following the client through to hospital admission, make sure you liaise closely with other staff, especially nursing staff. Keep them in the picture about what the client has been told.
>
> 2. Check out what the patient understands about their symptoms, establish their main fears and counter with full information where possible.
>
> 3. One of the issues which may be raised at this stage is the fear of death and dying. It is important to go along with this, but not raise it before the client does. A suitable entry to the subject is almost always provided by the client directly, or indirectly through discussion of making a will for example.
>
> 4. Try to help the client decide what they want to do, and what the issues are at this stage, for them and for those close to them.
>
> 5. If the client wants to raise the issue with family, discuss ways of breaking the news, either a bit at a time or all at once.
>
> 6. Try to find out whether there any practical difficulties at this stage which have not been broached, job-related, money-related housing-related, and so on.

Bridging

The rest of the book! This sort of work will use all your helping skills.

Warning

Remember to respect the client's wishes, though it may seem to run counter to good practice at times, for example with the hospitalised patient who does not wish their parents to know about their lifestyle, or the cause of their illness.

Intervention in suicide situations

I am including a session on the topic of suicide because trained helpers are sometimes in the front line when

- suicide is threatened
- the survivors of suicide try to cope with what has happened
- communities are faced with the trauma of a successful suicide.

Focus

The aim of this section is:

- to help you to develop appropriate confidence when faced with a suicide situation
- to develop your skills in identifying a potential suicide
- to focus on the skills of getting adequate professional and other support for the potential suicide client
- to suggest ways of helping family members when suicide has happened
- to help you learn skills for helping the community when suicide has happened.

Comments

This book does not make any attempt to focus on the causes of suicide, nor does it try to deal with the very important task of preventing suicide in your community by studying the causes.

Any threat of suicide must be taken seriously by the helper and by those persons in the client's support system. Those clients who take pills, or cut their wrists in an effort to make a statement intending to get attention for some real or imagined problem, sometimes have suicidal accidents. They die when they do not intend to kill themselves.

Because of the potential guilt feelings that one has contributed to a death, helpers and family members must *never* give in to any request 'not to tell anybody'. Anyone in the support system of a potential suicide person, has a right to support for themselves.

This is not only a right of the helper, it is a benefit to the client in suicide situations. The basic rules about confidentiality still apply. The survivors of suicide, including some of the professionals who have been working with the victim, are often in an emotional emergency for a time following a suicide. A whole community, when it is a small one, usually goes into shock and depression, which in itself is an emergency.

That community may well be the workplace, or an office within the larger work situation. The community itself needs emotional help. The skills outlined in Chapter IV on achieving a relationship, apply when taking steps to help the community work through the emergency.

Fear and helplessness are among the oppressive, strong feelings which emerge in the face of a suicide. These emotions are often denied. The result is blaming others or oneself for the death. Inappropriate anger results, and is mistakenly used as a way of avoiding the feelings of fear and helplessness. You will be helping the survivors and the community when you accept their fears and their feelings of helplessness. Such acceptance can be the first step toward better emotional health.

Once the crisis has abated, the normal working through of grief will take place. However, there may be some aberrations to the normal grief process. An individual or a whole family may slip back into a crisis and need additional support.

Illustrations

A. Arthur was in a severe accident two years ago, and ended up with some minor brain damage. He got retraining for his job as a book-keeper, and has been doing fairly well at work. Things at home haven't been going so well. His youngest son, aged 21, moved out to take a job in a distant town. His wife Sue has not been happy in the marriage for a long time. In the face of his growing independence and his ability to take care of himself, she has decided to leave him.

It is now two days since Sue left and took many of the household belongings with her to her new place. Arthur is devastated, and one of his first comments is, 'There is nothing to live for anymore'. He has been alternating between thinking about how he would end his life and blaming Sue for being an irresponsible wife. He tends to come out on the side of 'I'm no good any more since my accident.'

B. Janice is a 35-year-old woman who lost her only child in a swimming accident last summer, just after her daughter's eighth birthday. The weather has been bad for two months now, and Eunice has withdrawn from any family or community support. It is clear from the session, so far, that she plans to end her life by taking an overdose of pills she got a few days ago from her family doctor.

As the helper, you already have the details of her plan. Janice asks that you do not tell anyone.

Comments

The human tendency to blame, as a way of avoiding one's own pain, often adds to inappropriate guilt both on the part of the blamer and the one being blamed. There are several issues around guilt and forgiveness. Who forgives? What do you believe about forgiving yourself? What about making amends as a way of ridding yourself of guilt when the victim is dead?

What do you believe about the right of an individual to take their own life? Is talking about suicide or murder likely to increase its occurrence? Is it better to deny that suicide and murder happen? Giving serious thought to the above issues will benefit you and clients with whom you work when suicide is an issue.

Step by step procedure

1. Move immediately into talking about the reference to suicide. Acknowledge that you are aware that it came up and that you want to talk about it.

2. If the client denies that there was any talk about suicide, indicate your need to talk about it anyway. State that you are still not clear, and that you are concerned.

3. Once it is on the table, begin a careful pursuit of how the client would go about committing suicide. Let them talk and do not get involved.
   (a)   Simply listen with your best listening skills.
   (b)   Do not try to talk clients out of their plans.

4. *Tell* the client that you have certain steps you always take when faced with talk about suicide. Be clear about these steps. The steps should include:
   (a)   You will talk to a professional in the presence of the client. Get on the phone and permit the client to listen to your side of the conversation. Do not leave them alone in the room to go to a phone. Call a doctor or another person in the mental health field and report your concern for the client. Tell them that you need their help now. (Call the police as a last resort!)
   (b)   You do not take responsibility for the client's safety. Be clear with the client that you cannot take on that role, that the cards are in their hands, and are stacked against you. State that you care about them, and any others who are important to them.
   (c)   If their intentions are clearly thought out and serious, insist that you must follow through your plan of not leaving them alone. Insist that you approach some other competent person from their support system to become involved.

5 Before leaving the serious suicidal client, offer the following, providing you can follow it through. When they are troubled by suicidal thoughts in the future you are open to be one of the people available for a phone call to talk about these thoughts. (This is a serious responsibility and the helper must not be without a supporter or mental health consultant when making this offer, to avoid getting caught as the only person providing help.)

   Ask for a promise that they will call and talk to some other very specific helper when they get suicidal thoughts.

Warning

Never, never promise anyone who has threatened suicide that you will not tell anyone. And do not allow yourself to be the only helper involved in the client's support system.

Always consult a mental health supervisor when you are involved with a suicidal client.

Working with the depressed person

Almost everyone at one time or another experiences low periods, 'blue Mondays', and all of us know about sad feelings. Take two or three minutes to reflect on the last time you were in the presence of someone where the atmosphere was very heavy. You may have been with a person who was depressed. The most common emotional problem in our society is depression.

Focus

This section will help you to:
- distinguish between mild depression and an emergency
- develop skills that will enable you to take appropriate action in the situation
- develop skills that will enable you to support the depressed person, when and where appropriate
- learn the difference between depression and grief.

Illustrations

Ordinary depression

Bill has had a fear of growing old since he was about 30. A year ago he had a mild heart atack. He had good medical help. When he came back to work he got help from a professional about his anxiety over his work performance. He has exercised himself back to normal good health. However, there is one exception. He became depressed along the way although the doctors have reassured him that his heart will stand all normal activities.

Bill, in his depression, has isolated himself from his support system. He is endangering his marriage because of his negative attitudes toward life in general. He is talking with you because his wife insisted that he get help. As you talk he has revealed that he has given up most of his activities, e.g. cross-country skiing.

Acute grief

Alice went back to work three years ago when the youngest of her three children was ten. She had been a devoted mother and dependent wife. Her husband was buried four weeks ago, having died suddenly of a heart attack. She is now back at work. In her grief she is:
- blaming the doctors for his death
- talking seriously of leaving the children with her mother, taking a holiday and going away to an expensive resort for a month's rest. Her mother is not well. It is doubtful whether the money is there to finance such a trip
- complaining about heart pains and lying down frequently during the day until the pain 'goes away'.

Alice has three symptoms of acute grief, the most obvious one that of developing the same symptoms from which her husband died.

An emergency

Meg is a single parent who lost both her marriage and one of her two daughters some twelve years ago. She has been depressed for two months now. She does not have any idea why she is feeling so badly. However, both of you know that her other daughter finished secondary school two months ago and is moving out in another week. In the past two weeks Meg has been unable to cope with her job and has called in sick for more than half of the working days.

Comments

Depression is hard to identify. It is easier to identify acute grief (see p. 39). One of the difficulties in identifying depression is that often the cause is not known even to the client. Depression is usually related to serious losses, even though the client may not see the connection.

At other times depression is caused by an anticipated loss, such as anticipated dismissal or retirement from your job. Such a person may well become depressed weeks in advance of the event.

Sometimes depression may be caused by chemical imbalances, or poison. These imbalances may develop through prescribed or other drugs, or may result from some form of illness.

Some people are manic depressive. For the helper this means two things.
1. Manic depression tends to be an on-going emotional problem, which can be controlled by medication, but it is difficult to get rid of the problem altogether.
2. With manic depression the client moves through wide and severe swings of being very high and very low. These clients appear to be free of the problem when they are half way between the extremes of the cycle.

It is important that you are able to assess the difference between depression and grief. Normal grief is a difficult experience but is not an emergency. Acute grief on the other hand is always an emergency.

Grief and depression require a certain amount of time to work through the system. The average depression is over in three months, unless it's manic depression or the client is a persistently depressed person. Normal grief may take up to three years to work through.

Step by step procedure

There are five skills which are basic in providing help to the depressed person.

1. Make an assessment as to whether it is depression or grief.

2. Determine whether it is an emergency, using the guidelines above, the material on *Acute grief*, p. 39, and that on *When it's an emergency*, p. 28.

3. Make sure that the client has sufficient and appropriate people in their support system. Turn to the section on *Helping a client to develop external resources,* p. 98.

4. Confront the client to make achievable changes, using your best supporting skills.

5. Using gentle confrontation, encourage the client to return to manageable everday activities. In supporting and confronting the depressed person, you may need to take the person by the arm and encourage them to go with you to do something different, like going for a coffee. They sometimes have little energy for making that decision and acting on their own.

6. A very first step is to listen to and accept the clients' strong feelings. Let the client describe those feelings for you. See the warning opposite.

Bridging

Read the sections in the text on:

- *Helping the client build up external resources*, p. 98. and
- *Timing interventions*, p. 94.

Warning

While working with the depressed person we need to beware of a tendency to avoid or deny the client's feelings. Occasionally you will meet a depressed client who needs to be confronted about their habit of hanging onto the depression because of all the sympathy they have been getting. These clients will wallow around in their sad feelings and need firm, but understanding support in getting on with life.

Facing possible terminal illness

Focus

This section can be useful in developing skills that will enable the helper to respond to a client who is having difficulties because of the possibility that they have a terminal illness.

Illustrations

A. Gary, aged 54, works in the accounting department of a medium-sized firm. Six weeks ago he was diagnosed as having cancer, and the medical profession decided it was best not to operate. They told him that he had a better chance with a course of chemotherapy. He had a difficult time during the months that he underwent therapy. However, he is feeling great again, simply tires easily at times, and has been back at work for two weeks.

Mostly because they have not dealt with fears of their own death, his fellow workers are avoiding talking to him about his experience and fears.

B. Susan in her early fifties had a mild coronary. She is back at work and had been doing all the right things following such an attack. However, she is somewhat depressed and finds it hard to concentrate on her work. She had made comments indicating that she is afraid of dying. There is less likelihood that she will die of a heart attack now than before the coronary.

Comments

In most situations when the topic of death comes up there is an uncomfortable silence or someone quickly changes the subject. Many of your fellow workers will walk to the other side of the room rather than come face to face with someone who has a terminal illness. The same thing happens in grief situations. If they see a fellow employee coming towards them, they do not want to get into any serious conversation with that person.

The chief root of this discomfort is in the fact that most people, unless they are quite old or have faced death one way or another, have never thought seriously about their own death.

Other factors which get in the way of responding to somone who is or may be terminally ill are:
- lack of understanding for those under emotional stress
- lack of awareness that caring listening is far more important than the words used in talking with the terminally ill.

Individuals who are terminally ill or who fear their own death are sensitive to picking up the discomfort of other people. Hence they are slow or unwilling to open up the matter of their own concerns. The aftermath is increased loneliness and blocked emotions, both of which get in the way of any possible recovery. For those who will die within a short time, their journey will be more difficult and painful because of the blocked emotions and loneliness.

Recently, some hospitals and medical schools have started training nurses and doctors to be comfortable in talking with the terminally ill about death. It is quite possible that most family members and some close friends are having the same difficulty in responding to this need to talk and be understood. The chances are that one of your fellow workers who is afraid of dying is desperate to talk to an understanding, trained person like yourself.

Step by step procedure

1. The very first step is to think seriously about your own mortality. One way to develop some sense of ease with the notion of your own death is to talk with others, especially someone who has training in working with death and the dying. You may be able to find a workshop or brief course on the topic. Chaplains in hospitals frequently offer such workshops.

2. When you are with a terminally ill client you are talking to someone who has probably received the impression that it is not all right to talk about their fears of death. You will need to apply your very best listening and understanding skills. Listen for the message and respond with active listening. See p. 64.

3. When the door opens the client may develop strong feelings and avoid the question by changing the subject. Understanding is important at this step. You have to tread the fine line between respecting the client's right to remain silent and confronting the client's resistance. If you want to develop this skill, find a willing partner and practise the skills outlined in the sections on understanding, p. 68, and resistance p. 100.

4. As trust develops you can anticipate that the client will want to talk about one or more of the following:
   - anxiety about what will become of family members if and when they die
   - money matters
   - the fear of a painful and long drawn out illness
   - how they will go about preparing their partners (spouses)
   - tough decisions to make between continuing to work, or spending more time with their families and friends
   - all sorts of unfinished business that facing death brings up
   - concerns about life after death.

5. Although referral may well be appropriate in order to avoid getting out of your depth and to serve the best needs of your client, do not abandon them at the point of referral. There are too few people in everday life at work, in the medical field or at home who are comfortable in assisting the terminally ill person.

Warning

Whether or not the client is actually facing terminal illness, or is worried about death as a result of some past or recent experience, the emotions and concerns are to be treated equally seriously. You will find your own feelings more of a problem when the client is actually facing death.

Take care in developing an appropriate balance between confronting the resistance to talk further and not violating the client's rights and needs.

Marital and family break-up

The high incidence of separation and divorce in this country and many other parts of the world
- requires front line helpers in the workplace, in schools and in the community who are available when the situation takes on crisis proportions
- involves nearly every citizen because separation has touched their lives in some personal way. This personal involvement makes it difficult for many would-be helpers to be objective.

Focus

This section will help:
- to provide you with skills for identifying whether there is an emergency, when invited into some aspect of a marriage and /or family break-up
- to provide skills and self insight that will prevent the helper from getting caught in taking sides, and so contribute to a worsening of the situation.

Illustrations

A. Margaret's husband has just walked out leaving her with three small children. Her friend, Alice, called you because she was afraid that Margaret might commit suicide.

At this stage of the meeting you have already established that Margaret is in an emotional crisis. She has not combed her hair and has real difficulty looking you in the eye. There are no thoughts about suicide. Alice dressed and fed Margaret's children this morning after she arrived on the scene.

Margaret is putting all the blame on her husband, and is not very open to talking about her own feelings of helplessness, shame and fear. Margaret would feel and function better if she could allow herself to experience those feelings. The anger and the blaming are blocking off those feelings.

B. Jim and Eileen's marriage had been in trouble for three or four years. Eileen avoided the problems by isolating herself and fully devoting herself to their two daughters and one son, ages 7–12. Jim avoided the problems by complete dedication to his job as an accountant. His work situation was one where he made few friends. He had withdrawn from his current family as well as from his family of origin. He and Eileen had been staying away from social functions because of their troubled relationship. Eileen chose a time when he was near exhaustion at work to tell him to pack up and get out. He has just moved into an apartment with little furniture or utensils. Jim knows practically nothing about cooking, sewing or looking after a house. Eileen has encouraged him to take more things with him, but he was reluctant, because he was afraid of making it permanent.

Comments

A common device for avoiding one's strong feelings of helplessness and guilt is to blame. Anger and blame are used also as a way of not facing one's own part in the break-up. Because of these dynamics it is very difficult for friends, and some mental health workers, (including the helper) to be effective in supporting the person(s) in crisis.

For comments on identifying when it's an emergency, see p. 28. In particular, emphasise how important it is for the client in the emergency to have one person available who is strong and objective. This makes it doubly important for the helper to be aware of their own biases, unresolved feelings from the past, or fears about their own marriage and family. Self-awareness, together with supervision, may prevent a helper from making the situation worse. It takes discipline too!

Individuals, and even whole families, can go into a panic state in anticipating a major loss. I have worked with many people in an anxiety state over a feared loss of a partner. In these situations, one faces many of the symptoms associated with the actual loss. It is difficult to determine when in a marriage break-up you are most likely to find an emotional emergency. However, experience indicates that one of the worst times is around the actual physical separation, when one partner moves out of the family home.

Step by step procedure

1. If you are faced with a client similar to Margaret it will be important to:
   - be understanding without taking sides
   - listen for feelings as well as information
   - watch for any tendency you may have that would trap you into taking sides, such as fears about your own marriage breaking up
   - learn some of the important skills that are useful in these situations.

2. Study the case of Jim above and consider:
   - confronting Jim about enlarging his support system
   - methods of referring him for separation counselling
   - helping him to help himself in solving the practical problems he now faces
   - methods of suggesting to Jim that he pay attention to daily routine and ritual, as help for getting through his emergency.

3. It is important that you know what professionals are available in your area for either separation counselling or marriage and family counselling.

Warning

Do not try to work with any client where you are getting caught in the middle. Also watch for your biases. Most clients in the initial stages of a break-up look to you to be a judge rather than someone who will help them through their stress.

When a teenager runs away

Focus

This section will serve to:
- increase the helper's understanding of family dynamics when teenagers run away
- develop your skills in supporting family members
- explain what to do in helping families to help themselves in effective action.

Illustrations

A. Derek is the second son in a family of two boys and two girls. His brother Alec is two years older and is doing well in his last year of high school. Derek runs away after a mother-son fight which neither of them really understands. He goes to a large city some 100 miles away and finds a youth shelter he heard about on TV.

His mother had been a school teacher before the children arrived. His father is a successful accountant. They have always lived in the same house in a better than average part of town. Before he was born, his father became disillusioned with his marriage, and his wife sensing this latched onto her newborn son. Derek is 15 and he has not yet been able to cut the apron strings. She becomes very jealous of any girl that Derek looks at. The fights usually centre around his friends.

B. Sue is 16; her parents broke up four years ago. Her father had some alcohol problems, and found a girlfriend. Her mother was able to get custody of her three children. They haven't heard from their Dad for two years and do not know where he is living. Her brother, one and a half years older than Sue, replaced Dad as head of the family. The family has a history of 'triangling' – two against one. This happened a lot in the early years. Now Mum and brother Andy continually triangle against Sue.

Sue runs away when she discovers from her younger sister that Dad had tried to contact her two months ago, and Mum and Andy decided to tell Dad that Sue did not want anything to do with him. She had been longing to see her Dad again.

C. Jim is the eldest of two. He is sixteen and his sister is a year younger. His father drives an HGV and is away from home a lot. When he is home, father and daughter are very close; even Mum is left on the outside of this relationship most of the time. Dad has never been satisfied with Jim's achievements in school. In fact he has been critical of anything that Jim tries to do. Mum has tried to support Jim, but with little success when Dad is around.

Dad's firm has been on strike for two months now leaving him free to be at home a lot of the time. It's the school holidays and the exam results have just come out. Jim runs away without telling anyone where he has gone.

Comments

In most situations where a teenager runs away from home, the parent(s) focus on blaming people outside the family who influence and attract the young person. This tendency to blame arises out of the anxiety that develops in the situation. Blaming also has the function of permitting the parents to avoid facing their feelings of guilt.

The runaway may be escaping from an intolerable situation. But this is the exception rather than the rule. In most cases the runaway is either calling out for help, or making a strong statement about their unhappiness with the family situation. The family system has ceased to operate as it should.

The family is a system, which has a long history that reaches back into previous generations on both parents' sides. (There may be a history of family members, mum, dad, aunt or uncle who made similar strong statements by running away or in some other way.) The one who runs away disrupts the customary operation of the family system, however poorly that system may function.

In almost every situation the teenager is using a painful method of establishing their own identity. It is absolutely normal during the teen years to take steps towards becoming independent, your own person. In order to be a healthy, normal human being as you grow older, it is essential that you feel good about yourself. The family system often starts to break down when one or more family members are emotionally fused to another member. At times the strain of the fusion becomes so great the fuse blows and the circuit is broken temporarily. The fused family will make every effort to bring the runaway back into the system as it was. But this only ensures another painful break within a short time, or even worse, produces a teenager who never gets the opportunity to become a healthy separate person.

The family member(s) need to be helped to see the crisis as an opportunity to get help for making a much needed change in how the system functions. Yet the usual response in the anxious situation is for the family to tighten up and make every attempt to go back to the way things were prior to the runaway event.

The level of anxiety increases rapidly with the discovery that the teenager is missing. Usually, no one in the family knows where the teenager has gone. The uncertainty and feelings of helplessness add to the turmoil in the crisis. One or both parents may find it difficult to cope as they imagine the very worst happening to their son or daughter. Verbal fighting and blaming often develop at this point. The police are contacted prematurely, which makes it more difficult to reconcile with the teenager later.

Sometimes another family, who have been good friends of the family in trouble, get caught in the middle as they try to understand and provide refuge for the young person. They fear that if they tell on the young person, he or she will run off somewhere else where there is less security and support. If they are wise they will provide active listening and understanding as ways of encouraging the teenager to contact the family on his or her own.

As a trained helper you may be part of that other family, or your contact with the anxious parent(s) may have come through referral, your church or your place of work.

The support given and suggestions offered to the parent(s) by the helper can provide a real measure of help to the family in taking advantage of the opportunity open to them once the young person's whereabouts are known. As an outsider you are intervening in the system. Your interventions can:
- make matters worse
- support the family system in maintaining things as they were, and thus resolving nothing
- build on the intervention already made by the runaway, and help the family to turn a crisis into an advantage, so that everybody wins.

Step by step procedure

1. The very first step is to respond to the anxiety and fears of your client. Use your best skills in keeping the guidelines on pp. 64-65. Keep calm yourself, provide support and use understanding in listening to the verbal and non-verbal feelings. Listen for fear, guilt, anger, feelings of helplessness and confusion.

2. Check with your client to establish the size of their support system, and encourage contact with those people who will be helpful. Do not miss those people who know and possibly understand the missing person. The initial support needed by the family is from those who can help to reduce the level of anxiety and panic.

3. Once the client has settled down, take steps to get people in the support system working on locating the missing person. Have the parent(s) contact the police only if there is good reason to suspect foul play. Because there are so many reports of missing teenagers, the police will not begin action until the person has been missing for several days. Parents will tend to deny that there has been any upset at home prior to the runaway. They will often insist that running away is strictly out of character for their son or daughter, even when it has happened before.

4. By the time you become involved in locating the teenager, the parent(s) will have been on their own search. Most of their efforts will have been fruitless and only have raised their own level of anxiety. You can help by sitting down with them and assisting them in making a careful inventory of the most likely people to contact. If possible involve a teenage friend of the missing person.

5. Once the inventory has been developed, help them to decide on the best choice of person(s) to make each contact.

6. As a rule it is best for someone outside the family system to make the first contact with the missing person.

7. Another rule of thumb is that it is best to have the missing person initiate talking to their choice of family members.

Warning

Your responsibility, as one who has intervened as a helper, is not finished until you have done your very best to encourage the family to reach out for counselling with a focus on the family system. Discourage any effort on the part of a parent to treat the teenager as the one who needs help. The problem may be the marriage, or it may be a fairly common case of a family system that has broken down.

The importance of confidentiality

Your clients, like your closest friends, put their trust in you and confide personal information and feelings. They deserve complete confidentiality.

Focus

This section will serve to:
- impress on you the importance of keeping confidentiality
- help you become aware of some seemingly innocent traps.

Illustration

You have seen a 16-year-old daughter of an acquaintance. In her need to talk, she unloaded a lot of problems in the first session. You did not get round to telling her how you would handle confidentiality if her parents called. Her mother did call and all you told her was that you and Cathy got on well and that you expected her for another session. Cathy did not return. Although you did not break confidentiality, you had not made that clear to her during the first meeting. She was afraid of your telling her mother her innermost thoughts.

Comments

People who need emotional help have a need to share their feelings, fears and inner thoughts as well as to confess behaviour they would not report to others. In short, they need to be able to *trust* you.

There is the problem of what you actually do with the confidential information. Then there is the problem of what the client fears you may do or have done with it.

In any situation, such as in a company, where the client is accountable to others to whom you also have access, the situation is fraught with *real* and *imagined* dangers.

There are situations where some other person such as a spouse, parent, lawyer or the police may attempt to get information from you. They sometimes go after the information because of their own panic and may attempt to trick you into providing the information.

Helpers need to be clear themselves about their own principles and ability to keep confidentiality. They must inform their clients about their practice concerning confidentiality. With new clients, it is not enough to assume that they know without your telling them. Check to see if they are concerned on this point.

If for some reason you need to talk to another helper about the client, such as a family doctor or parent, be sure to get the client's permission; in writing is best.

If you have a colleague or consultant to whom you turn for help and/or from whom you receive training, inform your clients that you have this support. Do not ever put yourself into situations where you cannot turn for help. Assure the client that this is normal practice for you and that you will maintain appropriate confidentiality.

When I am in situations where I am contracted to provide any kind of report on the client, I follow certain principles and procedures. I tell the client that I don't like being in the situation and that I assume that by writing a report I am not put in a superior position to the client, rather it puts us in a position of mutual trust and support giving us a chance to assess progress. I am then able to respond to the client's feelings and opinions about the report in a helpful, caring and firm way. Although I do not permit the client to formulate the report, I show them the report, before I submit it.

Records

If you keep any records of what is shared in the meetings, your client should know about it. Furthermore, you should be able to assure your client with integrity that the records are not available to their family or superiors. If, in the client's interest, you have to share material from the records, make sure you have the client's permission. Trust can be developed and maintained when confidentiality is guaranteed.

Step by step procedure

1. Do not provide any unnecessary information when talking or writing about a client whether you are talking to the family doctor, the school principal, the probation officer, etc.

2. Get to the point and report what is essential.

3. Ensure confidentiality at all times.

4. Do not exclude the client from your report writing.

Bridging

This material on confidentiality applies to other relationships:
- close friendships
- colleagues at work
- workshops and seminars
- wherever people need to trust you in order to tell you about themselves and their emotions.

Warning

You cannot be too careful about confidentiality. Watch yourself closely for every urge within you to tell somebody. If you need to talk with someone to settle yourself down, follow the advice on p. 143 about the helper getting help.

When no one appears to need your help

Focus

This section covers the following situations:
- Qualified helpers volunteer their services and no one seems to want or need their help.
- There are potential clients with emotional problems and emergencies. Yet, there is no structure in the community to allow the client and helper to get together.
- The helper is 'only a volunteer' and does not feel that they have any authority. Hence the helper is shy about offering their services.

Illustrations

A. Albert has taken two courses in 'helping' prior to moving to a new area. Being new, he has lots of free time. He doesn't know where to turn in this new community to offer his skills.

B. Edna was called by a neighbour asking her to visit a friend whose husband had just left her and the small children. Edna's neighbour says that her friend is a very open person and it would be fine for Edna just to drop in without any formal introduction. By what authority does Edna make the visit?

Comments

There are several issues in these illustrations depicting some of the difficulties in getting together with potential clients.
- Some people think that they should be able to take care of themselves and do not easily ask for help.
- Some people insist on getting the best professional help and their first response is 'a volunteer is not good enough.'
- Helpers, particularly volunteers, often feel that they have no right or authority to be helping in this situation.

How to solve these problems

Training will assist the helper in understanding these problems and to gain skills in solving them.

In addition, or in the meantime, the helper should contact one of the local agencies or organisations that has a structure for arranging meetings between helpers and clients when the need arises.

The places to look for such organisations are:

Churches	Volunteer bureau
Local college	Social services

Step by step procedure

1. Read the sections in Chapter IV, Part 1 on achieving a relationship.

2. Give some thought to where your authority lies. Is it:
   - the authority that comes through a recognised agency on whose behalf you act e.g. MENCAP, your church, etc.
   - the authority within you because of your training, your skills and motivation to help others help themselves.
   - the authority the client gives you when they ask for help
   - the authority the client gives you when you agree on a formal contract of helping.
   - the authority the resistant client begins to give you as trust develops between you?

3. If you are a volunteer for a church or other agency, it helps if the sponsoring agency develops some means to let the community know that you act on their behalf, e.g. an article in the local newspaper or church magazine.

4. When clients say that they really want a professional, say something like, 'Maybe we can look together.' Do not argue in an effort to prove your worth. As you look together, you can still help and the client may just decide that you are 'good enough'.

5. When clients feel shy about asking for help, say something like, 'It's difficult for most people to ask for help'.

6. If there is no organisation in your community that brings clients and helpers together, go out and round up one or two other interested people. Then talk about ways to solve the problem. Choose the most likely people, such as:
   - other helpers.
   - people who have status in the community, e.g. doctors, clergy, councillors
   - people who appreciate what helpers can do.

7. Contact MENCAP or your vicar or priest. They will talk over with you about how you might go about solving the problem.

Bridging

Chapter IV, Part 1 offers help in establishing the relationship once you are in contact with a client.

Warning

Remember, as a helper it's quality and not quantity that counts. In *one* situation you may help someone to help themselves and life is forever richer for them.

The helper gets help

Your first responsibility as a helper is to yourself. You have a responsibility to attend to your own emotional life and to improve your skills.

Workshops and seminars will help with the skills, yet something more is needed in order to avoid getting stuck and/or emotionally exhausted yourself.

The very best model for looking after yourself is to have easy access to a competent and caring mental health professional. The idea of 'supervisor' in this field differs from what most people in business and industry understand to be the role of the supervisor.

The role of the mental health supervisor is that of providing support as an equal. The supervisor should have more experience and expertise than you. Remember though that you have some skills and lots of advantages that your supervisor may not have.

A good supervisor can be your 'wailing wall', your confessor, and your encourager.

You can expect your mental health supervisor to use the same helping skills with you as outlined in this book. If those skills are not at least as good as those outlined here, you need to get yourself a new supervisor.

If you are providing help for people who are on the same payroll as you, then your supervisor should come from the outside, or from some non-partisan counsellor employed by the firm. If you have to avoid getting support because you are afraid of losing your client's trust, you leave yourself open to pain, disappointment and exhaustion. In short, do not box yourself into any helping situation where you are not free to turn for help yourself.

Do not wait until you are stuck with a client or until you need urgent help yourself. When you first begin meeting with clients is the right time to line up your supervisor.

Look around among the following list of professionals and do not settle for the first one you talk to; pick the best person for your needs.

The following professionals are among those most likely to have experience and training as mental health supervisors and/or consultants:
- Psychologists
- Social workers
- Psychiatrists
- Hospital chaplains.

Another model for getting this kind of help and support is to form a group of people who can provide supervision for one another. If you go along this route, it is important to invite a skilled professional to the first meeting to help you get started. Furthermore, it is very important that you all work hard at keeping confidentiality. See the section on confidentiality, p. 139.

If you are having difficulty which you don't understand and the same difficulty tends to happen over and over again, you may need more than supervision. Find a competent helper and get your own therapy. You may have blind spots you are not aware of. Many of the most competent helpers have had their own therapy along the way.

Rewarding ending

Rewarding endings are to be cherished! The approach of 'helping people to help themselves' has proved to be very satisfying for those professionals, volunteers and semi-professionals who have learned the skills. You, as a helper, can be one of them. The satisfaction comes through:

- watching people develop
- watching people become stronger as they cope with their emotional struggles.

Some of the satisfactions come as surprises:

- a client's delight in discovering an inner strength
- a helper's delight in discovering that all you had to do was to be there as a caring person who shares the crisis.

There is currently a most important role for you in our society to help with

- maintaining a high level of mental health in your community
- improving the mental health of those people who suffer emotional pain and confusion.

That role will increase in the future. Some of the reasons for the increase are included in the section, *Why helping is important*.

If you look after your own mental health, develop your skills and know your limitations, you will experience rewarding satisfaction as you help people to help themselves.